D0052265

THE BRADSHAW GARDENING GUIDES

Get up to date on the most important developments in gardening technology — the newest machines, chemicals, seeds, gardening aids and methods — and profit from John Bradshaw's many years of experience at the same time. This all-new series is the definitive guide to the what, why, where and how of successful modern gardening in 16 fully illustrated volumes.

- The Lawn Book
- Growing Gourmet Vegetables
- Annual Flowers
- The Indoor Plant Primer
- The Complete Book of Bulbs
- Evergreens
- Perennial Flowers
- A Guide to the Balcony Garden
- The Shrubbery Book
- Growing Garden Fruit
- Roses
- A Guide to Children's Gardens
- Biennials for the Specialty Garden
- The Book of Trees
- The Landscaping Manual
- Controlling Garden Pests

John Bradshaw

The Lawn Book

How to Grow the Perfect Lawn

McClelland and Stewart

Copyright © 1982 John Bradshaw

McClelland and Stewart Limited
The Canadian Publishers
25 Hollinger Road
Toronto, Ontario
M4B 3G2

Canadian Cataloguing in Publication Data

Bradshaw, John, 1916-
  The Lawn Book

Includes index.
ISBN 0-7710-1550-X

1. Lawns. I. Title.

SB433.B72   635.9647   C82-094329-0

Design & Illustrations: Pamela Patrick/Anodos
Design Concept: R.K. Studios
Cover Photo: Malak
Author Photo: Nir Bareket
Special thanks to Dr. J.L. Eggens, Dept. of Horticulture,
University of Guelph and to Sid Page, U of T.

Printed and Bound in United States of America.

About The Author

Born in the famed Garden Belt of the Niagara Peninsula, John Bradshaw is today one of horticulture's best-known writers and broadcasters, as well as being one of the most widely travelled. His information is gathered first-hand from the major garden areas of the world. Every year he visits the bulb fields of Holland, the flower fields of California, the All-America Trial Grounds, the major meetings of the American and Canadian Nurserymen's Associations and the American Horticultural Council. His simple down-to-earth style of writing has introduced many beginners to the relaxing pleasure of gardening and television and radio audiences know him well.

Contents

You and Your Lawn

March and April

May

June

TEN BASIC RULES
FOR SUCCESSFUL GARDENING

1. Use the right tools for the job and keep them well-maintained.

2. Know your soil and condition it with the proper humus and fertilizer.

3. Plan your gardens and grounds well in advance of sowing or planting.

4. Choose the seed to suit your needs and your growing season.

5. Know your local frost dates and adjust your planting schedule to suit your climate.

6. Learn to recognize when and how much to water.

7. Cultivate to keep roots healthy and weeds in check.

8. Make sure the light conditions are right.

9. Know your enemies and eliminate pests or diseases as soon as they appear.

10. Use pesticides, fertilizers and other chemicals sparingly and carefully.

You and Your Lawn

Think of some of the most picturesque gardens you've seen in the past few years and I'm certain the one landscape feature which stands out in your memory is the rich green lawns that surrounded them. They were well fed, carefully graded, smoothly mown and a joy to behold.

More and more people are realizing that an attractive home surrounded by a bright green lawn is a veritable haven amid pollution, crowded streets and the tensions of the "rat race".

I look at the home and the garden around it as a living watercolor. The house is the subject of the picture, the flower beds, hedges, fences and other landscape features are its frame and the lawn becomes the background or wash.

In landscaping any property we're trying to blend the house and its architectural lines into the scenery as if it had always been there. That's why we surround it with a green lawn, plant shade and flowering trees and shrubs, add foundation beds and flower borders, and place hedges or fences around the perimeter of the garden. While all of these factors are important and necessary, the lawn is by far the most significant.

A smooth, well-cared-for lawn provides vital benefits both seen and unseen. For instance, the saleability of the house and property is increased considerably if there's an attractive lawn in first-class condition. Such a lawn can add thousands of dollars to the market value of the property at sale time.

Another major unseen advantage is the role a lawn plays as an anti-pollutant. Through photo-synthesis which takes place in its leaves, healthy grass is able to absorb carbon dioxide from the air and exchange it for the pure oxygen we all need to breathe for survival. The pores of the grass leaves are continually giving off oxygen; 25 square feet (2.25 square metres) of lawn is able to provide sufficient quantities to sustain an adult for 24 hours.

Not to mention that a rough brown lawn will greatly detract from the beauty of flower beds, trees, shrubs, and the remainder of the garden.

9

The current trend toward outdoor living means that we're using lawns much more than we have in the past. For the husband and wife with a young family a section of the lawn at the rear of the home can be used as a special play area for the children. This area is best separated from the rest of the garden by a low hedge or flower border. If the lawn is blessed with both a level section and a slope, make the sloping part the children's special area. Children have great fun and enjoyment rolling down grassy banks in the summer. Later, when the children are older, the area can be converted to a vegetable and fruit garden.

Keeping the lawn green and healthy is not difficult if you learn the basic facts of lawn care, and that's what this book is all about. The home gardener of today has it easy compared to a few years ago. There are many tools, powered and otherwise, including much improved lawn mowers, aerifiers, cyclone fertilizer spreaders, de-thatchers and powered rakes; we have new insecticides, fungicides, weed killers and lawn grasses, all of which combine to make the job of establishing and maintaining a first-class lawn simple and easy. Our grandparents would have been truly amazed and "green" with envy.

Know Your Soil

I doubt whether anyone can become a truly successful gardener without having a good understanding of soil. It plays a significant role in every aspect of gardening, from the creation of a first-class lawn to growing all types of indoor and outdoor plants.

What is soil? First of all, the particles themselves are actually pieces of rock created through the erosion of mountains over millions of years. But it's the humus, the billions of bacteria and other micro-organisms, and the plant food elements between these particles that constitute the major factor in the growth process of all plants and trees.

The difference between a light sandy soil and a heavy clay is merely a difference in the size of these particles. For example, comparing the grains which make up the two soils would be like comparing pumpkins to garden peas. In clay soils the minute particles are compressed together resulting in poor drainage and preventing the free circulation of vital oxygen. On the other hand, the larger particles in sandy soil carry oxygen, water, and the valuable plant food elements easily through the earth.

The answer to how you improve a heavy clay or a sandy soil that's too light is always the same. Start by digging plenty of humus into the earth just as soon as it becomes workable in the spring and repeat the process in the fall just before putting the garden to rest for the winter.

In a heavy clay soil the humus will encourage the minute particles to form larger clumps, substantially improving drainage and oxygen

circulation. When added to sandy soils, humus acts as a sponge, soaking up and retaining moisture and preventing the essential nutrients dissolved in it from being leached away.

In my grandfather's day, there was usually a plentiful supply of well-rotted barnyard manure readily available. The use of this manure was considered to be the ultimate answer to successfully growing all plants. However, the value of well-rotted manure of any sort has been greatly exaggerated. Within 24 hours fresh manure will have lost up to 90 per cent of its usefulness as a plant food. Soil scientists have now determined that cow or horse manure is only about 1.5 per cent

11

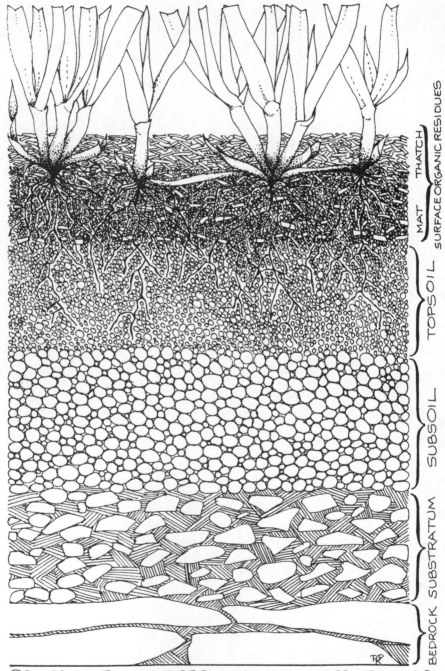

SOIL PROFILE UNDER TURF, SHOWING THE LAYERS OF LIVING & NON-LIVING MATTER BENEATH THE SURFACE (NOT IN SCALE).

nitrogen, whereas grass clippings from the average well-fed lawn will be about 2.5 per cent nitrogen. The home gardener will therefore use a combination of humus and a complete garden fertilizer.

A complete garden fertilizer will contain balanced amounts of 3 major ingredients — nitrogen, phosphorus and potash — plus valuable trace elements such as magnesium and iron. Nitrogen stimulates the green growth of the plants, phosphorus aids in root growth and enhances the color of flowers, fruits and vegetables, while potash promotes the overall health of trees and plants in much the same way as vitamins do in animals.

The key elements in successful gardening are water, plant food, sunshine and light, and plenty of humus. Unless your soil contains lots of humus, the effectiveness of the other 3 ingredients will be severely restricted.

Few people realize that the natural supply of humus is not inexhaustable. Every time you prune a branch, pick fruit, vegetables or flowers, or throw out grass clippings and leaves, you are effectively removing potential plant food and energy from the soil. If these vital materials are not replaced regularly, the earth will gradually lose its ability to sustain growth of any kind.

March and April

The home owner with an unsuccessful lawn usually dooon't feed it at all or at best gives it one feeding in the spring and expects this to do for the whole of the gardening season. It's true that one feeding in the early spring with a complete lawn fertilizer high in nitrogen can increase the growth of a lawn. Recent research over a five-year period showed that the average improvement was approximately 80 per cent over no feeding. I'm sure you'll agree that this is a significant increase but any home gardener can boost that figure to 180 per cent simply by emulating the greenskeeper of a good golf course. Long before the players arrive he'll be feeding and caring for the greens and fairways on a regular basis, from early spring until the middle of October.

A first-rate lawn requires a minimum of 4 feedings per season. Why does it need so many? The simple answer is that the well-kept lawn is the perfect mechanism for using up the supply of plant food in the soil. At least once a week during the growing season between one-third and one-half of the grass plants are removed by the lawn mower and, in most cases, consigned to the garbage. By removing these clippings you are also taking away one-third to one-half of the food manufacturing part of the grass plants. It's surprising for many people to realize that the **only** reason we mow a lawn is to keep it neat.

Even on those lawns where the clippings are allowed to remain, there's always a considerable loss of nitrogen and other plant food elements from the earth. This takes place because the trillions of soil bacteria require fuel to break down the clippings into valuable humus which will be readily assimilated by the earth. Nitrogen is the most important plant food element involved in this miracle of nature and can rightly be called the staple food of the soil bacteria.

First Feeding and Fertilizer

The time to give the lawn its most important feeding of the season is just as soon as the snow has melted, when the frost is out of the ground

MALAK

15

and the surface of the lawn has dried a little and firmed.

In warmer areas, where freezing of the ground is not a problem, the best time to give this initial feeding is the first week in March.

Such an early feeding is vitally important because otherwise the unfed lawn will actually be starving from that time until early May. As soon as the soil temperature rises above $32\,°F$ $(0\,°C)$ the grass plants begin to grow and are immediately in need of nitrogen. Any plant food remaining in the earth from the previous year will have been changed by nature from chemical into organic, or manure, form. The organic form isn't released to the waiting grass plants until some time in May when the temperature of the soil rises consistently above $55\,°F$ $(13\,°C)$. This permits the countless numbers of bacteria to start working and releasing the organic nitrogen to the grass plants.

In any successful complete lawn fertilizer the most important plant food element is nitrogen. The grass plants need at least twice as much nitrogen as any of the other plant food elements. Adequate nitrogen ensures excellent growth and the development of a rich dark green turf. But make no mistake about it, other plant food elements are needed as well. Phosphorus is included in any complete lawn fertilizer to stimulate root growth. Potash is a catalyst which acts like vitamins do in you and me, promoting the overall health of the grass plants. **For each measure of nitrogen applied to the lawn you also need to add approximately a half measure of potash.** A lack of this vital food element will mar the appearance of otherwise healthy grass. Persistent use of a lawn fertilizer which does not contain enough potash will eventually result in the lawn turf developing a condition which closely resembles root-rot in oats. This is actually the visible symptom of an acute potash deficiency in the earth.

In addition to the major plant food elements of nitrogen, phosphorus and potash, your fertilizer should contain some minor elements such as magnesium and iron. The latter is very important because it's essential to the chlorophyl production in the leaves.

Every package or container of fertilizer sold anywhere in the world always lists nitrogen first, phosphorus second, and potash third by numbers. For example, if you see the numbers 21-3-9 on the bag you'll know it contains 21 per cent nitrogen, 3 per cent phosphorus and 9 per cent potash. The remainder is composed of a neutral medium, through which the elements are evenly distributed.

In spite of its pleasures and satisfactions, gardening is often a rather frustrating and time-consuming hobby. As a direct consequence of this fact, home gardeners have increasingly come to welcome and use any products and/or methods which give quick results.

One of these products is nitrogen that is immediately available in the form of ammonium sulphate or ammonium nitrate. In the hands of the professional greenskeeper "instant nitrogen" is often used for special purposes, such as readying golf greens for tournaments. It's most unfortunate that many lawn owners are advised to use such chemicals for the first feeding of the lawn in the spring, in the mistaken belief that all the grass plants need at this time is nitrogen. Under no circumstances should these substances be used by an amateur. We've already mentioned that in the growing of grasses and grains, for every measure of nitrogen applied we also need to add approximately half that amount of potash. In addition to acting like vitamins, the potash is also a catalyst which enables the grass and grain plants to burn starch for energy. The more nitrogen you pour on the lawn the more potash is needed.

No one wants to go to the trouble of making a separate application of potash, so the only sensible thing to do is to use a complete lawn fertilizer high in nitrogen and containing balanced amounts of nitrogen, phosphorus and potash, together with such important minor or trace plant food elements as iron, magnesium, calcium, sulphur and boron.

The only successful and foolproof way of applying fertilizer to the lawn is with a good quality fertilizer spreader. Scattering it by hand or with a shovel is often disastrous with considerable and severe burning of the turf taking place. A good fertilizer spreader in proper working condition should be an important part of every gardener's collection of tools and machines. Home gardeners with small lawns can obtain the use of a spreader for a few hours from the nursery, garden center or hardware store where they purchase their fertilizer and other garden needs. Rent-all stores in the larger cities and towns also carry them. The best spreader to use is the cyclone type which distributes the fertilizer evenly over the surface of the lawn. In applying the fertilizer make sure to follow the manufacturer's directions to the letter.

Raking

After a long hard winter there's a natural and compelling tendency to want to get out in the garden and do something on the first warm spring day that comes along. For many people this takes the form of going to the tool shed or garage, grabbing a heavy sharp-toothed steel rake and giving the lawn a thorough combing, as if it were suffering from a severe case of dandruff. This is done in the belief that such a practice will help the lawn. Nothing could be further from the truth.

All that these over-anxious gardeners succeed in doing is to rake into a pile the valuable layer of humus built up from last year's grass plants and their clippings. Afterward, the pile is usually burned or consigned to the garbage can.

17

J.L. EGGENS

Early spring fertilization after 3 weeks. Brown area on left was not fed.

If the clippings had been left on the lawn sooner or later they'd have returned to the top inch or so of the lawn soil as a very valuable form of humus. One of the new mower mulchers gets around this problem by fine-cutting the grass clippings so that they fall to the surface of the earth and in 1 to 2 week's time are already entering the soil.

The only reason for raking a lawn in the early spring is to remove any sticks, stones, bones or other debris that could damage the lawn mower or give the lawn an unsightly appearance as it gradually turns green in the warming spring sunshine. Any raking given the lawn in the early spring should be done with one of the light-weight bamboo or aluminum rakes which are shaped like an open fan.

Rolling the Lawn

Another favorite early spring chore, carried out faithfully by many, is to go over the lawn with a heavy roller while the ground is still soft and oozy. The home owner decides that this is the ideal time to smooth out the bumps which were so apparent every time the lawn was mowed the previous summer. To accomplish this type of levelling, the man of the house fills a heavy roller with water and has a great time running back and forth across the lawn. I'll grant that this does smooth out quite a few of the bumps, but at the same time it creates untold damage to the lawn by turning its surface into an excellent imitation of a hard roadway. This practice is one of the major causes of soil compaction, a

18

J.L. EGGENS

Nitrogen-deficient turf.

much worse enemy of lawns than dandelions or plantains. Compaction jams the particles of soil so closely together that vital oxygen is unable to circulate freely and reach the roots. It also creates a run-off problem because rain or water from the sprinkler has difficulty entering the earth. Compaction goes a long way toward fatally weakening the structure of the roots.

Admittedly, there are times when rolling can't be avoided, such as when a perfectly level surface and grade must be created before sodding or seeding a new lawn. Frequently, even this is done with a heavy roller in such a way that it does more harm than good. There's enough compaction caused by the family's regular use of the lawn for recreation and other purposes without compounding the problem by using heavy powered or manual rollers during the making of a lawn or in the early spring.

A lawn that's only slightly uneven is best levelled in early May, or late August or September. It should be smoothed out with sterilized top soil which is now generally available in waterproof bags from nurseries, garden centers and hardware stores. This soil will have been specially treated to kill any weed seeds it may contain. First, scatter the sterilized top soil over the surface of the lawn and then push it from the high spots to the low ones with the back of a steel rake or with a metal doormat dragged back and forth over the surface by a rope.

For small hollows or depressions that are quite deep, you can lift the

19

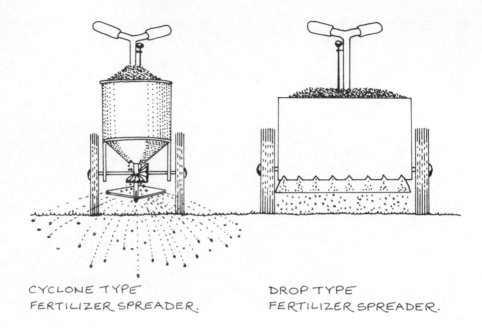

CYCLONE TYPE
FERTILIZER SPREADER.

DROP TYPE
FERTILIZER SPREADER.

sod with a shovel in early May, once the grass has started to grow vigorously, and fill in the hole with sterilized top soil. After carefully replacing the sod, tamp it down firmly with the back of the shovel until it's level with the surrounding surface of the lawn.

For high spots the best plan is to lift the sod with a shovel, remove the excess earth and replace the sod again. If the sod is carefully lifted in early May, while the weather is still on the cool side, the sod will not suffer any set-back and it will never know it's been moved. The ideal way to fill large depressed areas in the lawn is to gradually put down layers of sterilized top soil. Up to a maximum of 2 inches (5 cm) may be added at one time without danger of smothering or harming the grass plants. Starting in early May when the grass plants are growing vigorously you can add a new layer of sterilized top soil each month until the low spots have been entirely filled in.

I emphasize the use of top soil that's been sterilized, either by chemical or heat treatment, to kill any weed seeds. The surest way of adding dandelions, creeping Charlie, crabgrass and other annoying weeds to the lawn is to use unsterilized top soil.

Check your lawn for low spots in late winter or very early spring, immediately after a rainfall and while the ground is still frozen. The low spots will be filled with water which isn't able to drain away. Such spots are sensitive to disease and winter killing. Sometimes a rainfall will fill them with water just before the cold weather sets in. If this

20

moisture freezes and remains that way over the winter months it can smother the grass plants in the same way as the ice surface of a backyard skating rink would.

It's therefore very important to mark the low spots so that they can be filled in early May with sterilized top soil.

Greening Up the Lawn Ahead of Time

There's an easy way to green up your lawn 2 or 3 weeks early in all areas where the ground freezes in the winter. You accomplish this by first giving the lawn its most important feeding of the year in late March or early April. Follow up with an extra early mowing. All lawns would turn green much sooner if it weren't for the dormant top half-inch of the grass plants, the dead leaves and other debris which keep out sunlight and water. This prevents the grass leaves from producing the chlorophyl which the lawn requires to become green in color.

For this very early mowing the height of cut of your lawn mower should be raised so that it will just trim off the top half-inch of brown grass. Once that has been removed you'll find the sunlight will be able to reach the turf and materially speed up the production of chlorophyl, aided and abetted by the nitrogen released to the grass plants by the first feeding of the year.

Keeping Traffic Off the Grass

Each year in the very early spring there's a period of time when the earth freezes at night and thaws in the daytime and the surface of the lawn becomes soft and oozy. While this is happening and until the earth

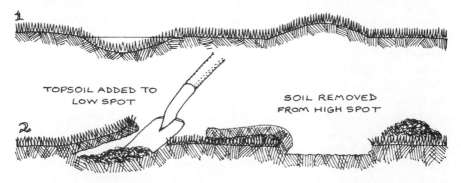

TOPSOIL ADDED TO LOW SPOT

SOIL REMOVED FROM HIGH SPOT

PROCEDURE FOR LEVELLING SMALL BUMPS AND DEPRESSIONS IN THE LAWN.

21

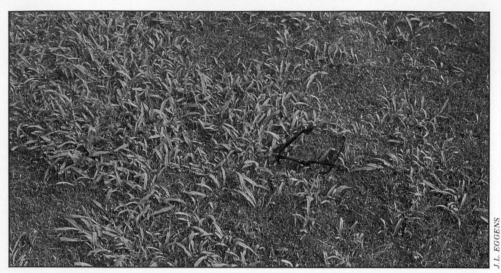

J.L. EGGENS

Crabgrass.

dries and firms, all traffic should be kept off the lawn. More harm can be done to the lawn at this time than at any time during the remainder of the gardening year. Don't let the children play on it, warn the postman and paper boy to stay clear, keeping everyone to the sidewalks or paths. Roping off the front lawn is often the only way of stopping traffic over it at this time of the year.

Early Control of Crabgrass

The worst lawn weed to control in eastern North America is, without a doubt, crabgrass. This weed has been aptly described as an invention of the devil, specially designed by him to plague home gardeners. More lawns are ruined each year by crabgrass than any other cause. You may lift your eyebrows a little at my calling crabgrass a weed. Keep in mind that the correct description of a weed is a plant out of place. Blue chicory, which is a noxious weed in eastern North America, is a cultivated garden flower in British flower borders.

Just a few years ago there was no control for crabgrass. It's an annual grass which only survives in the lawn from year to year because of its remarkable ability to re-seed itself. A single, well-developed plant can bear as many as 100,000 seeds. These lie on the surface of the lawn over the winter and start to germinate in May, just before the lilacs come into bloom.

Crabgrass can be a pest any year but it seems to be at its worst during summers that are hot and dry. It thrives on the same heat and drought that cause normal lawn grasses to run for cover.

22

J.L. EGGENS

Crabgrass [close-up].

While its leaves are broader and a lighter green than the desirable lawn grasses, it's difficult to distinguish crabgrass from the others until late July or early August. At that time the plants develop into matted patches which choke out the other grasses.

During the month of August the plants reach maturity and form distinctive and easily recognizable purplish seed heads which spoil the appearance of the late summer lawn and garden.

One of the real keys to success in controlling this vicious lawn pest is to mow the lawn twice a week during August and September. This will prevent the plants from setting the seeds that will assuredly produce more plants next year and the years that follow. The vitality of crabgrass seeds is amazing and they can last for 50 years or more and still germinate.

Crabgrass doesn't tolerate shade, so a healthy, thick, dense turf that is cut no shorter than 1-1/4 (32 mm), and preferably 2 inches (5 cm), is a big help in preventing the seeds from germinating and in retarding the growth of those that do.

Relatively high temperatures, moisture and light are the factors necessary for the seeds to germinate. The common practice of top dressing the lawn each year with unsterilized top soil provides the seeds with just such perfect germinating conditions. Crabgrass seeds which have lain dormant are suddenly given exactly what they need to germinate and infest the lawn. Unless the earth you use has been sterilized to kill the weed seeds, it shouldn't be used for top dressing the lawn under any circumstances. Sterilized top soils are easily available from

23

nurseries, garden centers and hardware stores. Alternatively, one of the composted cattle manures will also add vitality and thicken up your lawn without giving crabgrass, dandelions, chickweed, plantains and other persistent weeds a new home in your lawn.

Since crabgrass is an annual and the plants are killed each autumn by the first hard frost, our horticultural scientists realized that the logical way to control it was to destroy the seeds as they germinated. Up until the late 1950's most commercial products attempted to control crabgrass by selectively killing the growing plants. Many of these products would turn the surrounding desirable grass plants brown or seriously injure them. Still others were only partially successful, and grass specialists came to the conclusion that this method left much to be desired, especially because the seeds germinate over several weeks.

At long last a chemical was discovered that would kill the crabgrass seeds as they germinated and it has been successfully combined with complete lawn fertilizers high in nitrogen. One application of these combination lawn-care products will kill 90 per cent or more of the crabgrass seeds on the surface of the lawn. At the same time, you'll be giving the lawn its vital first or second feeding of the season.

In warmer areas, where it's possible to feed in March or in early April, the combination crabgrass preventer and lawn fertilizer should be used in the first 10 days of May and before the lilacs are in bloom. In the colder parts of the country where it isn't possible to feed the lawn early, the combination product can be applied in April to take care of the necessary first feeding and, at the same time, control the crabgrass.

There's another important plus. Regardless of whether you apply it to the lawn in April or early May you'll also be killing mouse-ear chickweed and many other grass or weed seeds lying on the surface of the earth. These seed-killing ingredients are highly insoluble, and if left undisturbed after their application will remain on the surface of the soil, preventing the germination of crabgrass and other weed seeds for 2 or more years. Here you have another excellent reason for not raking the lawn heavily in the spring.

Make no mistake about it: crabgrass preventers are like any other chemical product used in the garden and must be applied with care. I find that all too many home gardeners are careless in applying weed killers and fertilizers. Carelessness can often ruin the success of normally effective weed controls. Careful application is needed because the active ingredients which kill the crabgrass and other weed seeds as they germinate are insoluble. The rate of application must be very light. In order to provide the vital uniform kill over the treated area, every square inch of the surface of the lawn must receive a coating of the material. It must reach the surface of the earth where the chemical will become fixed on the soil particles and remain there as a thin coating.

No movement of the material occurs once it has become fixed on the soil particle. It won't move either sideways or down into the earth. Soil cores taken months after treatment have showed almost no penetration below the top 1/8 inch (3 mm) of earth.

Luckily, only crabgrass seeds on the surface of the lawn will germinate. It's not unusual to find many of them several inches deep in the soil but these will not germinate unless they're brought to the surface and exposed to light, moisture and warm temperatures. These seeds are not killed by preventive treatments since the chemical will not penetrate to that depth.

Whatever you do, don't guess at the rate of application. The lawn area to be treated should be accurately measured in square feet or metres. Then be sure to apply the combination crabgrass preventer and lawn fertilizer with a spreader, making your application no heavier or lighter than that recommended by the manufacturer.

My experience in our test gardens shows that it pays to set the spreader opening small enough so the combination product will cover the measured area twice, spreading half the material in one direction and then applying the remainder crosswise.

I'm sure all of these instructions seem to be a bit complicated, especially to the beginning gardener, but let me assure you that it's not nearly as difficult as it seems. Getting rid of crabgrass and other weeds in this manner is a big improvement over any other control used in the past.

May

The lawn probably requires more attention and care during the "merry month of May" than at any other time during the gardening season. This is the time for its second feeding of the year. For lawns that are free of crabgrass and insect problems use a complete lawn fertilizer high in nitrogen.

For those lawns that have already been fed in late March or in early April and that were troubled with crabgrass last year, the May feeding should combine a complete lawn fertilizer high in nitrogen with a crabgrass preventer. Crabgrass, mouse-ear chickweed and other annual weeds and grasses are killed as they germinate and at the same time the grass plants receive their second important feeding of the season.

Sod webworms, white grubs, ants and other insects often severely damage the lawn. Where insects are a problem another combination fertilizer product is available, this time combined with one or more insecticides. When applied in early May it gives the lawn its necessary second feeding and controls the insects at the same time.

In warmer areas it's also possible to control broadleaved weeds such as dandelions or plantains and give the lawn its May feeding at the same time, but I prefer to control the broadleaved weeds in early June. While the plant hormone which kills them, 2,4-D, starts to be effective when the temperature reaches 55°F (13°C), it really works best between 68° and 72°F (20° and 22°C). I use 2,4-D in the first 2 weeks of June, when the weeds are growing rapidly and the weather will have reached the latter temperature range on a daily basis.

Cutting the Lawn

May is the month when the grass plants in most areas start growing vigorously. After a few days of warm spring sunshine and a shower or two the lawn will need cutting for the first time. It's most important that you don't let the grass plants get too high before you make the initial cutting.

MALAK

27

Most home gardeners base the height of cut for their lawn on the way golf greens are cut. Nothing could be worse for lawn grass. Golf greens are planted with bent grass which is entirely different from the bluegrasses used for lawns. Bent grass, when correctly fertilized and watered, is able to produce an adequate leaf surface at very low heights of cut, often as low as 1/4 to 1/2 inch (6 to 12 mm).

Conversely, the new and improved varieties of bluegrass and fescue are best cut 1-1/2 to 2 inches (3.5 to 5 cm) high, with the odd exception. A lawn consisting of the popular Merion Kentucky bluegrass can be mown as low as 1 inch (2.5 cm) without trouble.

Low cutting for the majority of the grasses scalps them and removes too much of their leaf surface. This means that the remaining leaves will not be able to produce enough food to sustain satisfactory growth.

In the first flush of spring, when growth is vigorous and luxuriant, the lawn will probably need mowing twice a week for a while. **At no time should the amount of clippings removed be more than one-third of the total leaf surface.** It's better not to exceed one-quarter if at all possible.

Mowing wet grass should be avoided. Dry grass cuts more easily, doesn't ball up and clog the mower, and gives the surface of the lawn a much finer and neater appearance. Moreover, it takes less time to mow a dry lawn then it does a wet one.

The beginner to gardening should keep in mind that mowers are not built for grading purposes. Lawns that are a series of bumps and hollows will be continually scalped by the mower. The lawn should be re-graded so it can be mown correctly. At the same time, wear and damage to the mower will be reduced considerably.

Lawns cut regularly with power mowers sometimes develop a series of wave-like ridges at right angles to the direction in which they're mown, creating a washboard effect. You can prevent this by regularly changing the direction of mowing (diagonally or at right angles).

This is also the time of year when the home owner usually invests in a new lawn mower. I can't emphasize too strongly the need for buying the correct type and size of mower to suit your lawn. As in anything else in horticulture, it's better to buy on performance than on price. A good lawnmower may be expected to have manoeuvrability, ease of adjustment, durability and enough power for the expected use. The ready availability of parts and service is also an important consideration. The so-called bargain mower becomes the most expensive in the end if parts are not easily available and service is hard to obtain.

Tuning Up the Lawn Mower

The best procedure for the home gardener is to make the last mowing of the season in late autumn, when the grass plants have finally stopped growing, and then take the mower to the firm that sharpens and services it. During the winter months there will be plenty of time to have it sharpened and serviced correctly. Too many people wait until just before the first cutting will be required in the spring, when the dealer is already swamped with mowers and other tools in need of servicing.

For handymen who are able to service their own lawn mowers, the following suggestions will ensure easy starting and reliable performance during the lawn mowing season.

1. Clean the mower of old grass and accumulated dirt around the engine, the moving parts and cutting blades just as soon as you've finished the last mowing of the season. It will be far easier to remove debris then, with a wire brush or a kerosene-soaked paint brush, than it will be after the mower has lain around the basement, garage or tool shed all winter long.

2. Remove the spark plug and replace it with a new one. It's a small price to pay for peak performance throughout the entire mowing season.

3. Drain old gas and oil from the mower.

4. Clean the gas tank of rust and sediment after the last mowing of the season. Just before adding gas at the start of a new season check again for rust and sediment. Be most careful of rust resulting from gas that's been sitting in the mower all winter long.

5. Flush the crankcase by adding oil and running the engine until it warms up. Drain this oil while it's hot to remove the maximum amount of sludge.

6. Add new oil in the spring immediately before the first mowing.

7. Clean the air filter in the autumn by rinsing it in gasoline. Dip it in oil and replace in the mower.

8. Make sure the cutting blades are sharp and correctly adjusted. If not, see a competent local mower serviceman who can tune your motor to peak performance. He'll probably tell you that you should have two blades for a rotary mower so that one can be sharpened while the other is in use. The blade of a rotary mower will need sharpening once a month during the mowing season. Those of a reel-type mower should be sharpened before the beginning of the lawn-mowing season and again about the middle of July.

29

Safety Suggestions for Servicing the Gasoline Mower

- Do it outdoors because of the danger of gas fumes.
- Remove the sparkplug wire until ready to start the engine.
- Wipe gas and oil from the engine before starting.
- Make sure all nuts and bolts are secure before starting.
- Don't make any adjustments while the motor is still running.

Reel-Type Mowers

This type of mower is always recommended for cutting formal and semi-formal grass areas, including level, well-kept lawns and golf greens, tees and fairways. The cutting action of the reel mower is like that of a pair of scissors. Reels, when sharp and correctly adjusted, give a clean, even cut. Bent grass should always be cut with reel-type mowers.

For many lawns their use may be limited because they require relatively smooth and level grass areas on which to operate. They won't cut tall, rank-growing weeds and grasses. You'll also find that the cost of maintenance is somewhat higher than for a rotary-type mower. Reel mowers need sharpening before the mowing season starts and again in early July.

Rotary Mowers

This is the mower to choose for the average lawn, parts of which are usually on the uneven side. It can also be used under fairly rough conditions where control of grass, and in some cases weeds, rather than appearance, is the first consideration.

Rotary mowers are also useful for grinding leaves and grass clippings into a fine mulch which can be left on the surface of the lawn provided it's not so thick that it smothers the grass plants. Eventually it will enter the soil and become a source of valuable humus. Otherwise, it can be gathered up and used as a mulch for flowers, evergreens, fruits and vegetables, or added to the home garden compost factory. A rotary mower is also excellent for cutting tall, stemmy weeds in no-lawn areas, and for trimming the edges of flower borders and foundation plantings.

This type of mower cuts by impact, a cutting action similar to that of the old-fashioned scythe. For this reason a sharp, correctly balanced blade is needed to avoid tearing the grass blades and to prolong the engine life of the mower. The tips of grass leaves torn by the dull cutting blade of a rotary mower soon turn to an unattractive brown color. That's why it pays to have two blades rather than one, so that you can change to a newly sharpened blade each month of the mowing season.

The best lawn mower for the small or average size lawn that I've seen recently is a comparatively new electric model which not only cuts the grass but mulches the clippings at the same time. This mower has two blades which cut up the leaves of the grass plants so finely that they fall to the surface of the soil and in a week or two they're entering the earth. Very few lawn mowers that I've seen or used leave the surface of the sod in such a tidy condition.

Hand Mowers

With the current trend toward smaller homes and gardens there's many a lawn which would be better mown with a hand-pushed, reel-type mower. Modern mowers of this type are easy to push because of superior ball bearings. There's no noise pollution and your neighbor won't be calling you names if you mow the lawn early on a Sunday morning or at mealtimes. Also, the person mowing is doing healthy exercise. Hand mowers are much cheaper to buy and there are no fuel costs. These advantages, coupled with the current and continuing energy crisis, will no doubt mean that more and more people will return to using hand mowers.

Rules for Safe Operation of the Lawn Mower

Power lawn mowers have removed much of the hard work from mowing the larger lawn. Unfortunately, like many other labor-saving devices, they do present certain dangers. Some 5,000 Canadians and 50,000 Americans are injured each year by powered rotary lawn mowers and snow blowers.

The rotary mower can hurl a piece of wood, metal or a stone 80 feet (24 m) or further, at a speed of at least 200 miles (320 km) per hour. That's why it's so important that, before mowing the lawn, you make sure no objects are left lying about that could be picked up and hurled by the whirling blades of the mower. At the same time, see that children and other persons are not in the immediate area.

For the unwary and uninformed user these rotary mowers can, and often do, cut off toes and fingers. They propel debris that can plough deeply into flesh and bone with all the impact of .22 caliber bullet.

Injuries involving fingers and toes are usually caused by contact with the mower blades. Such accidents are normally triggered by the operator's attempt to adjust or clear the machine without shutting it off. Injuries from thrown objects usually affect the lower parts of the body, but if a person is standing some distance away, it's possible for the debris to strike any part of the body.

The most common foot injuries are caused by pulling the machine towards you or having your foot slip under it when operating on a downgrade.

31

A powered lawn mower is not a toy to be used by children or by careless adults. Often it's not the operator, but an innocent bystander who is hurt when an object is hurled by a carelessly operated lawn mower.

Depending upon whether the mower is gas or electric, it can present a fairly serious fire or shock hazard.

Most people operate a rotary mower year after year without doing any harm to themselves or other people by following a few commonsense rules.

1. Read the instruction manual carefully and know your machine thoroughly.

2. Shut off or disconnect the source of power before attempting to unclog the discharge chute or to adjust the mower from one level to another.

3. Work in daylight hours only, unless you have particularly good artificial light.

4. Keep children and other bystanders out of the working area.

5. Push, don't pull, the machine.

6. Stop the machine when it's going to be unattended even for a moment.

7. Be certain of your footing and balance, especially when using the machine on a slope.

8. On a steep grade, operate from side to side. It's easy to slip down into the machine or have it slide down on you.

9. Never allow children to operate a power mower.

10. Don't move rotary mowers across gravel driveways or walks while they're running. Gravel and small stones can easily become potent ammunition for the whirling blades which could bat out the dangerous missiles.

11. Always wear leather shoes and never mow the lawn while barefoot. Safety-toe shoes such as construction workers use are even better.

12. Don't wear long scarves or other loose-fitting apparel which can easily get caught in moving parts.

13. Before cleaning, adjusting or servicing your machine be sure to stop the engine. Disconnect the sparkplug wire on gasoline powered engines or unplug the power cord on electric mowers.

14. Never add fuel while the engine is running or is still hot from use.

15. Never use an electrically powered motor if the power cord is not in good condition and correctly grounded.

16. Always store fuel in an approved safety container and

remember that gasoline is a potential fire hazard in your home, garage or tool shed.

17. Correctly maintain the machine, frequently checking all fasteners, guards and parts. Built-in safety arrangements are effective only if they're in good working order.

18. Use extreme care on slopes when operating a mower that you ride.

19. As the various safety organizations point out, rotary lawn mowers are powerful machines and should only be operated by adults or responsible teenagers. Children lack the physical ability, the experience and the judgement to operate powered lawn mowers safely and are far too often hurt by them. Accidents involving rotary mowers usually result in serious injury. Keep them from happening in your family!

Danger to Trees

The lawn mower causes more damage to specimen trees and shrubs than any other source. For this reason it's wise to mow around trees with particular care. It also pays to surround each tree or shrub with a circular bed of earth at least 4 feet (1.2 m) wide. Such a bed will effectively prevent damage by the lawn mower, it will allow vital oxygen to reach the roots more easily and, when the trees are small, will make feeding much simpler. The lawn will also be considerably neater because grass plants seldom grow attractively and well right up to the base of a tree trunk.

In case the lawn mower does accidentally strike a tree, keep in mind that an ounce of prevention is worth a pound of cure where shrubs and tree wounds are concerned. A lot of decay can be prevented by removing any dead bark and painting the wounds just as soon as the damage occurs. Ordinary house paint will do if one of the special wound paints is not readily available.

June

There's still plenty of work to be done on the lawn throughout June, leading up to the start of summer. This is especially true for those lawns that are not in the best of condition. Almost any lawn should look presentable in May and during the first two weeks of June but once the big flush of spring growth is over the less healthy lawns will start turning brown and revealing other trouble spots.

The lawn will need another important feeding in early June. One that's in good shape with very few weeds showing on the surface should be fed with a complete lawn fertilizer high in nitrogen. A lawn infested with dandelions, plantains, creeping Charlie and other broadleaved weeds should be treated with one of the combination lawn fertilizer and 2, 4-D products. This will provide the necessary June feeding and rid the lawn of broadleaved weeds at the same time. Contrary to popular opinion, 2, 4-D is not a poison but a plant hormone which is absorbed through the pores of the leaves and is distributed through the entire plant. It causes the broadleaved weeds to grow so fast they die, approximately 10 days to 2 weeks after application.

Some time in June the home gardener will need to get the hose and sprinkler and begin watering the lawn once a week.

Repairing Bare Spots

Bare spots are always a problem for the home gardener to overcome. Here's a method of repair that I've found very satisfactory over the years.

First of all, loosen the earth in the bare spot with a garden fork, Dutch hoe or steel rake. Next obtain a bushel (35 Litres) or more of sterilized top soil from a nursery, garden center or hardware store. To each bushel (35 L) add 1 pound (400 gm) of a complete lawn fertilizer high in nitrogen and the same amount of the best grass seed mixture you can buy. I recommend you use one of the comparatively new coated seeds which will go unnoticed by the birds and is coated with phosphate

MALAK

35

assist the young grass plants as they germinate. Thoroughly mix the soil, seed and fertilizer together with a shovel. I find that a good place to do the mixing is in a wheelbarrow.

Enlist a friend's help. Work together with one of you throwing a handful or two of the mixture over the bare spot while the other lightly scuffs the surface of the soil with a garden rake. Leave any loosened dead grass on top of the soil to act as a mulch. Immediately after sowing give it a good soaking with the hose. Unless it rains be sure to keep the earth moistened for the next 5 weeks. Many of the better lawn grasses take up to a month to germinate. If you let the earth dry out thoroughly even once, the grass seeds may never germinate. The smaller bare spots can be prevented from drying out by covering them with used burlap bags until the grass starts to germinate.

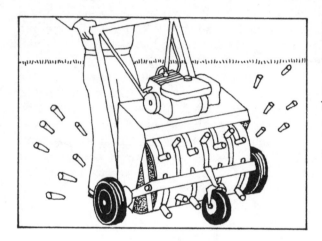

DRUM-TYPE CORING MACHINE FOR AERATING COMPACTED TURF.
IN DRY WEATHER, DRENCH THE AREA A DAY IN ADVANCE TO SOFTEN THE SOIL.

Thickening Up the Lawn by Aeration and Feeding

Some time in early June the home gardener usually finds his spring planting chores are just about finished. This means he can turn his attention back to the lawn which, by the middle of June, will have finished its springtime burst of growth and will be in need of some additional care and feeding.

The shortened work week has provided everyone with much more leisure time. As a result the lawn is used for outdoor recreation of some kind almost daily, from spring through summer to early autumn. This increased use means that the soil becomes much more compacted than in the past. Such compaction prevents the vital oxygen from circulating freely between the particles of earth. Compaction is especially serious on lawns created in clay soil. In cases of severe soil compaction

36

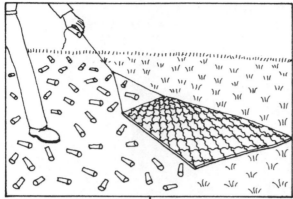

CRUMBLE SCATTERED CORES BY DRAGGING A WIRE DOORMAT OR A PIECE OF CHAIN-LINK FENCE BACK AND FORTH OVER THEM.

THE AREA CAN BE TOP-DRESSED WITH A MIXTURE OF PEAT-MOSS AND LOAM. THIS CAN BE FORCED INTO THE CORE HOLES WITH THE BACK OF A RAKE. THEN FERTILIZE AND WATER THOROUGHLY.

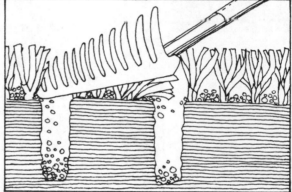

much of the fertilizer and moisture applied to the lawn either doesn't reach the roots of the grass plants at all or doesn't reach them in sufficient quantities.

One of the best ways of helping lawns that have become compacted is to aerify them. Golf courses have always been plagued with this problem, especially on greens. Greenskeepers solve the problem of compaction by using an aerifier machine to cultivate the surface of the greens. Similar machines, either powered or hand-drawn, are readily available for home lawn use. For the larger lawn an aerifier is one of the essential garden tools, along with the lawn mower, cyclone fertilizer spreader, rotary tiller and others. For smaller lawns, aerifiers can be rented when needed from one of the rent-all dealers found in most cities and towns. Also, custom aerifying can usually be found by looking in the classified advertisements of the daily newspapers, the large weeklies or in the yellow pages of the telephone directory. In our test gardens we have found that the hand-drawn aerifiers seldom, if ever, do a satisfactory job.

37

Repairing bare spots.

1. Injured turf.

2. Seeded and top-dressed.

3. After 2 months.

MALAK

J.L. EGGENS

38

The powered machines move over the surface of the lawn removing plugs of earth approximately 4 inches (10 cm) long and 1/2 inch (12mm) wide. Unless an aerifier machine is capable of extracting plugs of that size it's not really worth buying or renting.

These soil plugs are deposited on top of the turf. You might think this would create an unsightly mess. Not so. All you need do is to run a small wire doormat or the back of a steel rake over them and they'll easily crumble and fall in between the grass plants. They are thus returned to the surface of the soil. The holes created in the process of aerifying will allow the vitally needed oxygen and plant food to reach the waiting grass roots.

39

As soon as you've finished with the aerifier and the wire doormat or rake, apply a complete lawn fertilizer high in nitrogen at the rate recommended by the manufacturer. Then get out the sprinkler and water the lawn thoroughly so the fertilizer soaks into it. When you do this the nitrogen and other plant foods are immediately carried down to the grass roots through the holes made by the aerifier. In a number of cases I've seen a 30 to 40 per cent improvement 3 weeks after aerifying and feeding in this manner.

The modern fertilizer spreader does an excellent job of evenly applying the plant food to the lawn at the desired rate. However, trouble can occur at the turns. Unless you shut the spreader off just before you start to make a turn you'll place double the amount of plant food at the sides and ends of the lawn. This often results in serious burning of the sod at these points even when the sprinkler is turned on right after applying the fertilizer.

Watering the Lawn

Many home gardeners never quite get the hang of watering a lawn. Every summer I see any number of people sitting on the front steps or standing on the sidewalk and lazily sprinkling the lawn with the hose. Let me warn you, the garden hose is a very poor device for applying water to the lawn. So much time is needed to apply enough moisture in this manner that the job is almost always incomplete. Quite often when you water this way the surface of the lawn quickly becomes supersaturated. Once this occurs any further water will simply run off instead of being absorbed by the earth.

A famous horticultural teaching institution once made an enlightening test to illustrate this point. Small cans were placed underneath the sprinkler and the students were found to be applying 1/8 to 1/4 inch (3 to 6 mm) of water instead of having it penetrate the earth for 5 or 6 inches (13 to 15 cm).

There are many types of sprinklers on the market and many of them share a common defect: they spray in a circle. When the sprinkler is moved to cover a new area, either the circles overlap and waste water or they don't even touch certain areas and leave dry spots.

Although usually more costly in the beginning, sprinklers that oscillate and can be set to cover a rectangle are cheaper in the end. They spray the water from side to side, thoroughly covering a rectangle. In addition, they can be adjusted so they'll cover either a full rectangle or just half of it.

There are also underground watering systems made up of plastic pipes installed in the turf by making a slit with a spade. They have fixed sprinkler heads that will spray in a square. Such systems are

40

controlled by a single valve and a timer located at the house and take all the labor out of the important and otherwise demanding job of watering a lawn. During prolonged dry spells, when watering should be restricted to certain hours, the timer can be set to come on late at night or early in the morning.

In laying out an automatic sprinkler system, observe one major precaution: don't try to make a single head cover too wide an area. If the water pressure drops during a hot dry spell (or for any other reason) and your system has the heads spaced too widely, there's no way of watering the space where the patterns fail to meet. The best plan is to install the heads so they cover the area at 3/4 pressure so that opening the valve just a little will quickly compensate for the drop in pressure.

The biggest mistake made in watering is to give the surface of the lawn frequent light sprinklings. This is a most serious error which encourages the grass roots to grow close to the surface of the lawn where they're easily injured by a combination of hot sun and dry weather. Furthermore, this is the type of watering which stimulates the growth of crabgrass and other annual grasses.

The wisest and best rule to follow is to give the lawn a thorough soaking once a week. To be effective, the water must penetrate the earth to a depth of 6 inches (15 cm). I find 2 hours with an oscillating sprinkler set in one position is the correct length of time to ensure adequate watering.

During a severe drought it's often necessary to give a good soaking twice a week if the lawn grasses are to be prevented from going dormant. The bluegrasses we use for lawns are all cool season plants, and they'll go dormant without extra water when the weather is hot and dry. If this happens when you're away on a holiday or a business trip, don't worry, this dormancy is not particularly harmful although you probably will not like the brown, dry appearance of the lawn and there could be quite an invasion of weeds.

I don't believe that many people are aware of the fact that water can be applied to the lawn too quickly. When this happens, a layer of mud forms just at or under the surface of the soil. This layer soon becomes super-saturated and none of the water applied from then on will be able to penetrate the earth and will be lost down the drains.

Early to mid-morning is the ideal time to water a lawn, but any time during the day which allows the lawn to dry out before nightfall will be satisfactory. During hot dry spells there will be less evaporation if the water is applied in the late afternoon. A lawn should not be watered in the evening because prolonged dampness during the night, especially from the first of August on, will encourage the development of the fungus disease powdery mildew.

41

Nitrogen-deficient lawn.

I find the best way of ensuring that enough water is applied to penetrate the soil the required 5 or 6 inches (13 to 15 cm), is to place two large juice or coffee cans within the spread of the sprinkler. When the containers are filled with 4 inches (10 cm) water, the correct amount will have been applied.

Swimming pool water can be injurious to lawns and gardens if the level of chlorines and other disinfectants accumulated in the pool water is high enough to harm the grass plants. Taking everything into account, I think it's best not to use swimming pool water for the lawn or the rest of the garden. If you do, experiment with it on a small area

Patches of fertilizer burn.

42

Early drought symptoms. Grass turns dark green to blackish green.

J.L. EGGENS

first. Eventually, there can also be the problem of chlorine and other chemical salts building up in the soil. No harmful effects may be apparent in the beginning, but there could be a serious long term effect.

A New Lawn in the Summer

The couple who move into a new home in late May or June will most likely settle for a sodded lawn. It takes a real expert to sow grass seed and get a good lawn during the hot months of the year. Nevertheless, there is a way of seeding a small lawn successfully at that time of the year. Excellent germination can be achieved by gently watering the seeded area immediately after sowing and then covering it with old burlap bags. This method will not only prevent the newly sown seeds from drying out quickly but you'll be able to keep the soil moist by sprinkling the bags every day. At the same time, there's no danger of the seeds being disturbed by the force of the water.

Emergency Lawn

The best times to sow a new lawn are the last 2 weeks of August and the first 2 weeks of September. People who buy a new house in the late spring seldom want to go through the first summer with the daily possibility of soil being carried into the house by adults and children alike. There's a fairly easy solution to the problem.

First of all, you prepare the earth as you would for seeding or sodding a new lawn. Begin by scattering a complete lawn fertilizer high in nitrogen over the area at the rate recommended by the manufacturer. On top of this spread a 3-inch (7.5 cm) layer of humus. Composted

43

cattle manure, discarded mushroom manure, horse manure that's a year old, peat moss, or material from the home-garden compost factory are all satisfactory forms of humus to use for this purpose. The kind you choose will probably depend on its cost and availability.

Pick up a rotary tiller at a rent-all store and run over the area to be seeded 2 or 3 times. This will not only thoroughly mix the earth, fertilizer and humus down to a depth of 6 inches (15 cm), but will also leave it in a flour-like condition that's easy to rake. Rake 2 or 3 times and rough grade, making sure that the earth slopes gently away from the foundation walls to the sides, front and back of the garden.

After raking and removing any debris, you're ready to sow the same oats as the farmer uses. These may be obtained from any country feed and seed store. Sow the seeds thickly and then rake them lightly into the earth. In a very short time the seeds will germinate and when the new oat plants are 3 inches (7.5 cm) high, you should start cutting them as of they were regular lawn grasses. From then on, until the last 2 weeks of August, you'll be able to treat your emergency lawn just as if it were a permanent lawn area. Whenever the oats get 3 inches (7.5 cm) high, mow them again. Let the oat clippings fall to the ground where they'll be returned to the soil and provide a valuable form of humus during the preparation for a permanent lawn in late August or early September. Any time after the middle of August spread another 3 inches (7.5 cm) of humus, some extra superphosphate and a complete lawn fertilizer high in nitrogen over the prospective lawn area at the normal rate. Run over it again with a rotary tiller 2 or 3 times, rake several times to level and remove debris and you'll be ready for seeding or sodding the new lawn.

Lawn Weeds and Grass Problems

Annual Bluegrass [Poa annua]

In the 1980's there's a serious problem in many lawns which has been gradually getting worse over the past few years. Patches of *poa annua*, otherwise known as annual bluegrass, are now being found in many lawns. In the spring it's apple green in color and soon produces an abundance of low-growing seedheads.

When you first see *poa annua* in the lawn it's rather attractive and few people worry about it. As is often the case, looks can be deceiving. Make no mistake about it, annual bluegrass is a major pest and one of the most difficult to control. Being a narrow-leaved grass, it cannot be controlled by 2,4-D, the plant hormone which does such an effective job of keeping dandelions, plantains and other broadleaved weeds out of the lawn.

Another problem is the fact that annual bluegrass quite closely resembles Kentucky bluegrass, our most widely used lawn grass. However, it's lighter in color, doesn't produce underground creeping stems called rhyzomes, and is only 2 inches (5 cm) high at maturity.

Poa annua is correctly called an annual but in many respects it behaves more like a short-lived perennial. Its seeds germinate in the fall, survive the winter and grow whenever the air temperature rises above freezing.

One of the real problems in controlling this annual bluegrass is the fact that in the spring a crop of seedheads as long as 1 inch (2.5 cm) can be produced and can give the lawn quite a white cast. The seeds ripen and are responsible for re-infestation each year. Soon after the seeds ripen the plants usually die, leaving the seeds to perpetuate the problem.

You may well ask, if this type of grass is so attractive, why isn't it desirable in the home lawn? *Poa annua* has several major faults. It has a very shallow root system and it's short-lived. Normally the plants die quickly when the weather turns hot and dry, leaving large brown patches in the lawn. This is often puzzling to the home gardener when his once-green lawn suddenly becomes most unattractive.

The seeds of this annual bluegrass usually germinate in the late summer or early fall. It's also true that some germination will take place throughout the growing season during rainy weather. The large number of seeds produced and the extended germination period make this pesky nuisance difficult to control even when using one of the crabgrass preventers which has been combined with a complete lawn fertilizer high in nitrogen. However, a spring application of such a product in April or May followed by one in early September will go a long way toward eliminating this unwanted grass.

For a healthy, thick lawn that's been fed well on a regular basis, it's a good plan to use a power lawn rake (also called a dethatcher) to remove the excessive build-up of grass leaves. A heavy thatch will prevent the pre-emergence chemical lawn fertilizer and water from reaching the surface of the soil.

Poa annua has much less chance of getting a foothold in a lawn that has been given the correct care. A yearly aerifying to eliminate compacted soils, a good soaking once a week with the water penetrating the earth to a depth of 5 or 6 inches (13 or 15 cm) and feedings 4 or 5 times a year, will certainly discourage this bothersome grass from invading your lawn.

The height you mow the lawn is very important as far as *poa annua* is concerned. When a lawn is cut too short, its vigor is reduced and this gives the annual bluegrass a stronger foothold. There you have another

J.L. EGGENS

Annual bluegrass (poa annua).

important reason for mowing the desirable bluegrasses to a height of 1-1/2 to 2 inches (38 to 50 mm).

Annual bluegrass is like crabgrass and grows best in compacted soils that are supplied with plenty of surface moisture. The home gardener who sprinkles his lawn a little every day is just asking for trouble from this grass.

When brown patches appear because of *poa annua* dying out it's always wise to reseed or resod with a top quality lawn seed mixture. I like to use the same formula as recommended for filling in bare spots, mixing a bushel (35 L) of sterilized top soil, a pound (400 gm) of a complete lawn fertilizer high in nitrogen and a pound (400 gm) of the best grass seed mixture you can buy.

In early June the lawn grasses will be growing rapidly, especially if they were given a feeding with a complete lawn fertilizer high in nitrogen the first week in March in the frost-free parts of the country or just as soon as the frost was out of the ground in the colder areas.

This is also the time to take care of one of the most significant lawn problems. In the warming June sunshine the golden heads of dandelions will proclaim the presence of this pesky weed in the lawn. Until the introduction of 2,4-D the only way you could get any kind of control over dandelions was to dig them out, and this was seldom satisfactory. Now that we have first-class lawn fertilizers which have been combined with two or more types of 2,4-D, the control of dandelions, plantains, creeping Charlie and many other broadleaved weeds in the lawn is no longer a problem.

46

As I mentioned before, 2,4-D is not a poison but a hormone that is absorbed through the pores of the leaves into the life stream of the plants, causing them to grow so fast they die. A few years ago, when 2,4-D was only available in spray form, you had to wait for a very calm day before applying it. Now that it's been combined with complete lawn fertilizer we no longer have the problem of 2,4-D shifting with the wind to harm many other nearby broadleaved plants. However, one word of caution. In applying this material with a spreader you still have to ensure that none of the material falls on nearby flower beds or foundation plantings.

You should always wait until there's a forecast of at least 24 hours of dry weather and an air temperature of anywhere from 68° to 72°F (20° to 22°C). When the air temperature reaches 55°F (13°C) 2,4-D starts to work, but it works best around 70°F (21°C) and doesn't seem to work at all when it's over 80°F (27°C).

Common chickweed.   *Mouse-ear chickweed.*

Chickweed

A great many lawns each year are plagued by two kinds of chickweed: one known as "mouse-ear" and the other as "common". Until

47

very recently the only effective remedy was to ruthlessly pull out the plants as they formed.

The common chickweed is actually a winter annual which does most of its growing in the late fall, in winter under the snow, and in the very early spring. It's a proven scientific fact that the seeds don't begin to sprout until some time during the winter, often when the ground is covered with snow. Every time the temperature goes above $32\,^\circ$F ($0\,^\circ$C) the young plants start growing and keep on doing so until the temperature once more falls below the freezing point.

When spring has truly arrived, the common chickweed is in full bloom and often sets seeds before most home gardeners have taken any steps to get rid of this noxious lawn weed. Even this early in the season it's far too late and next year's crop of seedlings is already a certainty.

Any time during the fall, in the winter when there's no snow on the ground, or in the very early spring, I'd suggest that you examine your lawn and others in the neighborhood for patches of bright lettuce green which will be quite conspicuous against the brown of the dormant grass. A close look will show that these patches consist of prostrate plants with tiny oval-pointed leaves. These are the seedlings of the common chickweed.

At the same time you may notice plants that are colored a darker pinky-green, and which are quite similar to the common chickweed except that the leaves are oval in shape and have no point. If the leaves are held against the light, you'll find that they're covered with tiny white hairs. These are the leaves of the mouse-eared chickweed which is not an annual but a true perennial. It also grows actively during the mild spells of winter in exactly the same manner as the common chickweed.

Both of these lawn weeds can be controlled by 2,4-D. Again, it's best to use one of the combination products consisting of a complete lawn fertilizer high in nitrogen and one or more forms of 2,4-D. When you apply these materials, temperatures should be around $68\,^\circ$F ($20\,^\circ$C) to $72\,^\circ$F ($22\,^\circ$C) for effective control.

The common chickweed, but not the mouse-eared variety, is also killed by the same combination product used for controlling crabgrass. Such products not only kill the seeds of the annual chickweed as they germinate, but the annual weeds and grasses as well. Needless to say, they'll not harm the regular lawn grasses. The best time to make the application is during the month of September. The pre-emergence chemical that controls the chickweed will cling to the particles of soil over the winter and be ready and waiting for the annual crabgrass seeds in the spring, no matter how early they form and drop to the ground.

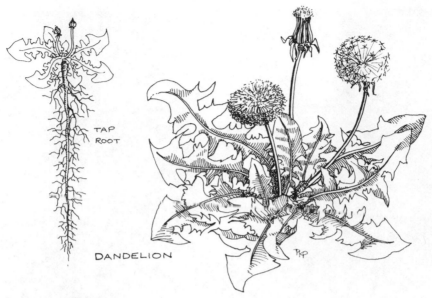

TAP ROOT

DANDELION

Common Pests

Dandelion

The most common and persistent broadleaf weed to infest the lawn is the dandelion which originally comes from Europe and Asia but is now found growing in most temperate countries. It has become such a widespread problem that there's hardly a lawn anywhere which doesn't contain some of these plants. The rosette of fluffy yellow flowers is familiar to everyone.

It's exasperating and frustrating for many home gardeners who have gone to considerable trouble freeing their lawn of dandelions, only to find it re-infested the following year from neighboring gardens, street sides or fields. What this really means is that dandelions must be controlled annually.

Quite often, in the late spring, you'll see people on their hands and knees in the lawn, grubbing out the plants with a knife or small hand cultivator. I hate to say it, but this is a complete waste of time. Dandelions develop deep tap roots several feet long and are capable of producing new tops from any portion. It's virtually impossible to get rid of them by pulling or cutting the roots just below the surface of the soil.

Even if you cut a root with a sharp knife several inches below the crown you'll not kill the plant. Two new heads will develop from the root, producing plants which will soon be as vigorous, or more so, than

Plantain.

the original plant. It's true that repeated cutting below the ground will exhaust the root reserves and the plants will eventually die. This primitive method is only practical on a very small lawn inhabited by very few dandelions. Moreover, the holes that are created are not only unsightly but give other weed seeds a chance to germinate and grow.

The best control for dandelions is to use one of the complete lawn fertilizers high in nitrogen which have been combined with one or more forms of 2,4-D. Make the application in early June when the air temperature is 68°F (20°C) to 72°F (22°C) and when the weather will be dry for at least 24 hours.

Often a second application will be needed during the first 2 weeks of August. There are also special combination products to feed the lawn until it stops growing in late November or early December (or later in warmer areas). They also contain other plant food elements that actually winterize the grass plants in much the same way as antifreeze does your car. The 2,4-D they contain works well when the temperature is 55° to 60°F (13° to 16°C).

Plantain

Sooner or later most lawns are also plagued by the common and buckthorn types of plantain. Both are perennials which cover the lawn from year to year. The common type has quite broad leaves while those of the buckthorn are ribbed and much narrower. The spiky seedheads

50

are stubby in the buckthorn, tall and slender in the common variety. Both form rosettes of dark green leaves. The plants die in the center, leaving a ring of small offshoots to grow the following year.

Both kinds cause the most trouble in lawns that are poorly drained and unfertilized. Unlike dandelions, isolated plantains can be successfully eliminated with a knife or hand cultivator if one cuts well below the crown. However, the easiest and best method is to use one of the combination 2,4-D and complete lawn fertilizers high in nitrogen at the same time as you control the other broadleaved weeds.

Creeping Charlie.

Creeping Charlie or Ground Ivy

These are but 2 of the more than 50 common names used to describe this lawn pest which is the hardest of all to kill. The plant has round, scalloped leaves, wiry stems and quite attractive lilac-purple blooms. In shady areas it has vigorous growth and makes a handsome plant, so much so that under those conditions it makes quite an attractive and useful ground cover.

In the lawn, however, it's nothing but a nuisance and of all the broadleaved weeds is one of the most highly resistant to chemical control. An application of one of the combination 2,4-D and complete lawn fertilizers high in nitrogen in June, followed by a second dose a month later, usually knocks it out of the lawn.

YARROW

Yarrow

The fern-like leaves of this perennial lie flat on the ground when the lawn is mowed and the plants definitely spoil its appearance. Just as soon as the young plants appear it's time to apply one of the combination 2, 4-D and complete lawn fertilizer products. You'll find that yarrow is easily killed in this early stage. The older plants develop quite a resistence to 2,4-D and 2 or 3 applications may be needed to kill them.

OXALIS

Oxalis

More and more lawns are being hit by this yellow-flowered perennial. I find that it arrives in lawns either through unsterilized top dressing or in the soil dropped from annuals at planting time. The plants are low growing with a pale green clover-like foliage which closely resembles miniature shamrocks. The yellow blooms are produced in clusters of 5. You'll find the leaves are quite sour to taste. The oxalis is easily eliminated at the same time, and in the same way, as you kill dandelions and the other broadleaved weeds.

J.L. EGGENS

Black medic or yellow trefoil.

Black Medic or Yellow Trefoil

Here we have an annual that produces thick, strong roots with stems trailing along the ground. The yellow blooms closely resemble those of peas or beans. The foliage consists of three small oval leaflets. A 2,4-D product, combined with a lawn fertilizer applied in early June, will easily control it.

J.L. EGGENS

Quackgrass.

J.L. EGGENS

Quackgrass [close-up].

Quackgrass

Quackgrass is the worst lawn pest of all. It is a virulent perennial weed, spreading seeds and underground rootstocks. Many people confuse it with crabgrass. Frequently, in the last 2 weeks of May, someone will tell me that they applied a pre-emergent crabgrass preventer in April or early May and the lawn is still infested with all kinds of crabgrass. As soon as they say this I know the culprit is quackgrass and not crabgrass. The latter starts to germinate just about the time the lilacs are in bloom and doesn't really show up until early August when the purplish seedheads mar the appearance of the lawn.

It's true that the leaves of the quackgrass plants do resemble those of crabgrass but they're easy to tell apart. Crabgrass leaves are a softer and lighter green while those of quackgrass have sharp edges which can easily cut you. These are the blades you used to place between your thumbs and blow on when you were a child, creating a very satisfactory rude noise.

If there are only a few quackgrass plants in the lawn you can dig them out by hand, although it's doubtful that you will be able to remove all of the underground rootstocks and they'll usually come back

55

to haunt you. A regular once a week mowing will help prevent seedheads from forming. Where there's a heavy infestation you have to decide either to live with it or to re-lay or re-seed the lawn. There are no selective chemicals which will eradicate perennial weed grasses such as quackgrass without killing or seriously damaging the desirable lawn grasses. Quackgrass is a very vigorous grower which resents the amount of mowing that a well-maintained lawn receives. Over a period of 2 or 3 years most of it should gradually disappear from a lawn that has been given regular and correct care.

Many people are not willing to wait this long for the quackgrass to disappear and, fortunately for them, there are biodegradable chemicals which will kill all the grasses, desirable and otherwise. In 48 hours you can safely seed or sod a new lawn.

MONEYWORT

Moneywort

Here we have the only common creeping weed with five-petal yellow blossoms. In some parts of the country it's also called ground ivy but there's no trouble in identifying it by the yellow blooms. Again, the treatment is the same as for all broadleaf weeds: a combination of 2,4-D and a complete lawn fertilizer high in nitrogen. One application in July will control it.

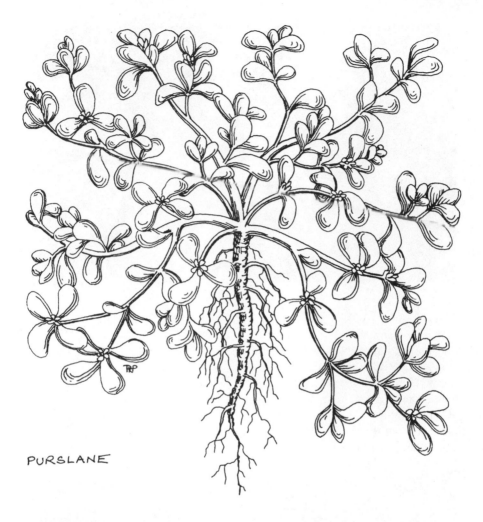

PURSLANE

Purslane

We don't normally think of an annual as being much of a lawn pest because the plants are killed with the advent of the first hard frost of autumn. Nonetheless, this persistent annual is becoming more of a problem with each passing year. Like most other weeds, purslane gets started in the lawn either when unsterilized soil is applied as a top dressing or when some soil from annual plants spills on the lawn at planting time in late May or early June. The stems are branching and lie prostrate along the ground. They're a smooth, reddish color and fleshy or succulent in texture. The leaves are broad at the tips. The same control as used for dandelions and plantains will quickly eliminate the purslane plants.

Mallow.

Mallow

In mallow we have a round-leaved biennial with tap roots. A biennial is a plant whose seeds germinate one year, the resulting plants surviving the winter and the following year producing blooms and seeds then dying. The stems of the plants trail along the ground, branching freely with alternating leaves. Pinkish or white colored blooms cluster in the axils of the leaves. Mallow is easily kept in check with the same combination products as you use to control dandelions and other broadleaved weeds.

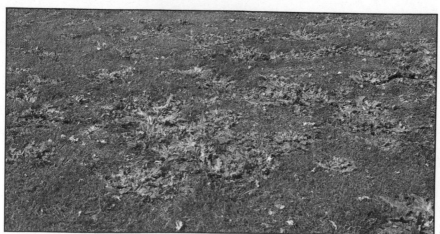

Thistles.

58

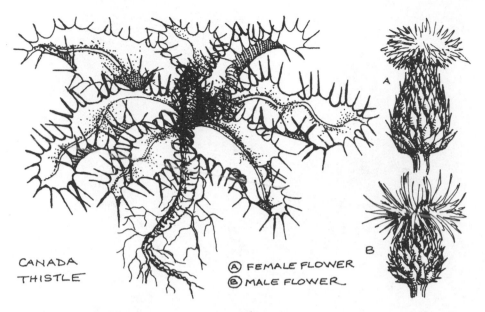

CANADA THISTLE

(A) FEMALE FLOWER
(B) MALE FLOWER

Canada Thistle

This perennial spreads quite rapidly from an extensive creeping rootstock. The purplish seed heads appear on top of 4 foot stems. Eliminating it by hand is almost impossible because of the prickly foliage and the way it spreads around each plant. For the latter reason alone it's wise not to let a substantial infestation occur. The June application of 2,4-D and a lawn fertilizer is usually all the control that's needed.

Chinch bug damage in lawn.

59

YELLOW FOXTAIL

Yellow Foxtail

Beginners to gardening may have trouble distinguishing yellow foxtail from crabgrass, which it resembles. However, unlike crabgrass, it doesn't creep. Soft foxtails appear in late summer. The same pre-emergence crabgrass preventer applied in September, April or early May will kill the foxtail seeds as they germinate.

Chinch Bugs

Many lawns these days are facing serious attacks from the chinch bug, a pesky little insect about 3/16 inch (5 mm) long. It starts to emerge from the egg stage of its life cycle in late June and for the next 6 or 7 weeks attacks the crowns of the grass plants by literally sucking the life out of them. Damage to lawns can be tremendous. I lost half of my own lawn to chinch bugs recently and had to replace it.

Evidence of hard attacks in eastern North America began to appear in the late 1960's and early 1970's with the attacks spreading and the

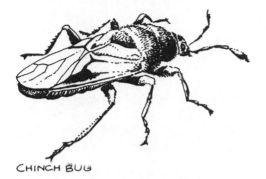

CHINCH BUG

ACTUAL SIZE OF CHINCH BUG.

damage becoming heavier each succeeding year. Nonetheless, those of us who live in eastern North America are more fortunate than gardeners living in Florida, who must contend with no less than 5 species of chinch bugs. We only have the hairy type to worry about at the present time. Lawns created on lighter sandy soils seem to be the most vulnerable.

The damage caused by an attack of chinch bugs begins to show up as brown patches which, unfortunately, closely resemble those caused by hot weather and drought. They gradually enlarge as the bugs move from one grass plant to another. The only sure way for the home gardener to tell if it's drought or chinch bug is to take a large juice can and remove both the bottom and the top. At the edge of the brown spot push the can an inch (2.5 cm) or so into the earth, filling it up with water. If the red-colored chinch bugs are present they'll float to the surface where they're easily recognized.

They normally start to actively damage the grass plants the last week in June, so that's when you should initiate control measures. The lawn can be given a thorough spraying with diazanon at this time but I prefer to use one of the combination insecticide and complete lawn fertilizers high in nitrogen. This way you'll be giving the lawn its July feeding and also controlling the chinch bugs, ants, white grubs and other insects that attack the lawn.

The seriousness of the chinch bug attacks at the present time suggests that consistent efforts to control them must be made every year during the last week in June or the first week in July.

61

July

The Lawn and Your Vacation

How can a lawn be left for 2 or 3 weeks while you're enjoying a well-earned vacation? The best solution is to hire someone to do the necessary mowing and watering while you're away. However, all those eager teenagers who were around looking for summer jobs earlier in the year have somehow faded into the shrubbery and cannot be found.

Give the lawn a short "crew cut" the day before you leave and chances are, unless the weather turns abnormally wet for this time of year, it will still be a manageable length when you return. Even if it's longer than normal don't worry, it won't hurt. The most important rule to follow is not to try to cut it back to the normal height of 1-1/2 to 2 inches (3.5 to 5 cm) right away. Instead, go over the lawn with the mower set high enough to remove about 1/3 of the tall growth. Two days later, after the grass plants have had a chance to recover from the shock of mowing, adjust the height of cut down to the normal 1-1/2 to 2 inches (3.5 to 5 cm).

If you're following the regular lawn fertilizer program which calls for a feeding the first week in July or August, omit it before you leave and make the application right after you return. This will also reduce the amount of growth you'll need to remove when you return. The odds are that a reel mower won't be able to cope with the extra-long grass. If necessary, borrow a rotary mower from your neighbor or obtain one from a rent-all store for this first cut-back after returning from a vacation.

Fairy Rings and Mushrooms

The more frequent rains of late summer and early autumn often encourage the growth of fairy rings and mushrooms in the lawn. What do we mean by fairy rings? They're not always true rings, although the uniformity with which they spread from a small central core is amazing. When you first see them they're intriguing and not unattractive. They

MALAK

63

begin as a bright spot of vivid green and expand outwards, a few inches the first season but often gaining speed as they spread. At the outer ring of the circle the grass is normally a vivid emerald green color, surrounding a zone of paler yellow or dead brown grass. Sometimes, the inside of the ring shows the same vigor as the outer rim but it can also be weaker in growth. When several rings occur in the same area, they can run together to form an irregular figure with scalloped edges. In many cases the ring will begin to fade to a weak, pale green as it advances and expands. At times it will grow inward as well. Mushrooms, sometimes mistakenly called toadstools, later appear in the outer ring.

There are many illusions and much false information about fairy rings and the mushrooms that appear in them. Down through the centuries, fairy rings have always had a great deal of superstition connected with them. In both Holland and Denmark they were supposed to mark the place where the devil churned his butter. In France, entering a fairy ring was said to produce a loathsome toad with protruding eyes which had the ability to cast magic spells. The Irish believed that the rings were places where the fairies danced, hence the origin of the common name.

Some say that the mushrooms which accompany the formation of the fairy rings are deadly poison. Others claim that they're harmless but inedible, while still others suggest they include some of the most delicious of all fungi. In truth, over 40 different species have been known to form fairy rings. They range from the highly edible Meadow Mushroom to the deadly Destroying Angel. Whatever you do, never assume that mushrooms growing in this manner are safe to eat.

Recent research reveals that the cause of stimulation and then repression of grass growth in the fairy rings is the underground, root-like structure of the mushroom which is correctly called *mycelium*. The fungus must have undecayed or partially decayed vegetable matter to serve as a source of starches and sugar. It grows and thrives on buried organic matter. Many fairy rings appear after the removal of elms which have been stricken by Dutch elm disease. The dead root system of a tree or the buried leaves are digested by the *mycelium* and in the process are broken down into the protein which is a rich source of nitrogen. This nitrogen acts as a sugar fertilizer on the grass and stimulates both root and top growth of the grass plants. Just as soon as the protein is exhausted the grass quickly fades.

Even more important, as the *mycelium* dies and no more mushrooms are formed within the ring, it creates a water-tight felt pad about 8 inches (20 cm) below the surface. This prevents normal moisture and food movement in the soil above the pad and the grass plants growing inside the ring are starved for both food and moisture.

Most treatments in the past were not too effective. Fortunately there's now a way of checking the problem, using one of the root irrigators which work so well on trees and shrubs both for feeding and watering purposes. Attach one of them to the end of the hose, thrust the tip 10 inches (25 cm) below the surface of the lawn and turn on the water. Keep applying the water until the sod lifts or puffs slightly indicating that the felt pad has been broken. Repeat the treatment around the entire circumference of the ring.

Next, thrust a drive fork into the ring all the way round and then pour in a solution of all-purpose fungicide. It is sold by a number of manufacturers under their own trade names and is generally available from garden centers, nurseries or hardware stores.

Although mushrooms appearing in fairy rings or on the rest of the lawn are difficult to eradicate, they'll eventually disappear when all of the organic matter in the soil has been used up. Knocking them over or picking them when they appear in the lawn helps to keep them under control.

Once the mushrooms in a fairy ring have disappeared the grass within the area of the ring often turns yellow and can be confused with a fungus disease. To correct the problem, aerate the ring with a digging fork, fertilize the area with a complete lawn fertilizer high in nitrogen, and then water the plant food into the earth with the sprinkler.

The only harm caused by mushrooms that appear indiscriminately in the various parts of the lawn is in spoiling its appearance. A little agricultural limestone over the areas where mushrooms are appearing seems to control them quite well.

If you know your mushrooms you may find that some of those in your lawn are non-toxic and make good eating. A major word of warning, if you *don't* know your mushrooms, *don't* eat them under any circumstances.

Control of Ants

By early July lawns created on sandy soils will almost always have some ants making a home there. Ants are famous for being among the most persistent of all insects. Sometimes their hills or nests seem to swarm all over the lawn. I doubt if you will be able to eradicate them completely, but you can cut their activity down to an absolute minimum.

Ants have a short life cycle, so they can repopulate any lawn in a hurry. They also tend to spread from one nest to create another and start new colonies. You've probably seen winged ants flying. At this stage in their life cycle ants do most of their travelling.

Ants are also hard to get rid of because of their adaptability. They

Fairy ring.

Mushrooms.

can survive in almost any kind of environment and they like such a wide variety of foods that there's hardly a lawn, particularly those made in light sandy soils, that is free of ants.

There are two reliable ways of controlling them in the lawn. Where there's a minor infestation, with only a small number of hills, each one can be dusted individually with a 5 per cent chlordane solution or some other special chemical. For large attacks use one of the complete lawn fertilizers high in nitrogen which has been combined with one or more insecticides. You'll not only control the ants but chinch bugs, white grubs, sod webworms and other lawn insects.

The 5 per cent chlordane dust is best applied in granular form, directly on the nests, using 1/2 teaspoon per hill. When applying the combination lawn fertilizer and ant preventer make sure you follow the

66

manufacturer's directions to the letter. For maximum effect let it soak in by applying enough water from the sprinkler to penetrate the soil for 5 or 6 inches (13 or 15 cm). Be sure to keep children and animals off the lawn until it has dried thoroughly.

During the hottest, and usually the sunniest, month of the year the home gardener who is proud of his lawn will give it another feeding with a complete lawn fertilizer high in nitrogen to make sure the grass plants don't go dormant and start turning brown.

In most other months, a good soaking once a week is a must if the lawn is to stay green. Any rain that falls during July, however, will normally come from thunderstorm activity. The chance of an all day soaker will be minimal. This means that during July you'll need to give the lawn a good soaking twice a week, instead of the normal once a week watering. The moisture should penetrate the earth to a depth of 5 or 6 inches (13 or 15 cm).

Brown spots that enlarge and persist despite liberal use of the sprinkler and feeding with a complete lawn fertilizer high in nitrogen should be checked for chinch bugs.

Shaded Lawns

By early July the trees will have produced their most dense growth of the season. Lawns which come close to, or surround, large shade trees will need extra care, watering and feeding.

Can a successful lawn be grown in shade? If the area is in full shade all day long, the answer is a resounding No!

Where someone has tried to grow a lawn for 2 or 3 years, either by seeding or sodding, without success, it's high time to recognize the fact that there just isn't enough sun for the grass plants. If you take a light meter and compare the light in a normal sunny area to a shady area and the latter has 25 per cent or less foot candles than the former, no one, no matter how dedicated, will ever succeed in growing a satisfactory lawn under such poor light conditions.

Our scientists and breeders have made some progress in developing special grasses that will grow as well in the shade as the regular lawn grasses do in full light and sunshine. Nevertheless, in such situations the shaded area is much better planted with one of several hardy ground covers.

For one reason or another, many people feel that the use of a ground cover as a substitute for lawn grass on a shaded area is an admission of failure. They feel that sown or sodded turf is the natural and right covering for bare earth. In reality, it's exactly the opposite. There are no plants that grow under more artificial conditions than do those that are used to make up a lawn.

The use of a suitable ground cover is merely sensible. No permanent grass will survive under heavy shade conditions. Even temporary or annual grasses are unable to last for a full growing season where many ground covers not only survive but thrive. I've always felt that well-cared-for plantings of ground covers were infinitely preferable to and much more eye-appealing than the best lawn you could hope for in the shade. Ground covers should be looked upon as a sign of the competent gardener, not as a confession of inability.

One of the biggest problems with ground covers until recently was controlling weeds among them. It's an unfortunate fact of gardening life that many of the common weeds are able to more or less thrive in subdued light conditions. They can be killed or prevented with new chemicals which, if carefully used at the recommended rates, can be sprayed directly on them without doing harm to the surrounding ground cover.

Broadleaved weeds and annual grasses can be stopped before they start by applying one of the new pre-emergence preventers annually. Application should be made just as soon as the ground becomes workable in the spring. It will kill most of the grass and weed seeds as they germinate but will not harm established plants such as any of the ground covers.

Ground Covers

Ajuga or Bugleweed

One of the best of the ground covers is ajuga or bugleweed, an aggressive grower that spreads rapidly. Buy 25 plants this spring and in 3 or 4 years you'll have 300. This is a quality that should be possessed by every ground cover. There are several types of ajuga, all of them having small lavender blue flowers. However, we do not grow them for the quantity and quality of the blooms they produce but for the attractiveness of their foliage. In addition to plain green, there's a rich maroon variety, one colored cream and pistachio green, and a red and yellow striped variety. They can be planted in patterns or in contrasting colors, creating extremely fine landscape designs.

Vinca Minor

Vinca minor makes an excellent ground cover. It quickly forms a dense mat of clean, glossy-green foliage that will eventually hide the soil completely. In late May or early June the plants produce quantities of lovely lavender blue flowers which are most attractive indeed.

68

Thorndale Sub-Zero Ivy

Another better than average ground cover is the Thorndale sub-zero ivy, really a special strain of English ivy which is not only a delight to the eye but, as the name implies, will withstand extremely low winter temperatures. It's a descendant of a remarkably hardy parent plant which came through over 25 Chicago winters without protection. When planted in the garden the Thorndale ivy is a strong and vigorous grower.

Japanese Spurge

The Japanese spurge or Pachysandra is a fine, dense-growing, evergreen ground cover for use in shaded locations where grass won't grow. The plants spread quickly by underground stems. They grow up to 12 inches (30 cm) in height and carry attractive glossy green leaves. White blooms appear in the late spring which add to its desirability as a ground cover. Pachysandra grows best in good soil containing plenty of humus.

Hosta or Plantain Lilies

Another happy solution to the problem of what to grow in the shade is provided by the hostas or plantain lilies. They're permanent and hardy and also bloom in July and August. The plants bear small white, lilac or lavender colored bells in one-sided clusters up their stems. They also need planting in soil that contains plenty of humus. The plants are vigorous growers and need setting 18 inches (45 cm) apart in the beginning.

Once established, they require almost no care. Pests don't attack them, severe cold doesn't affect them and they won't wilt even in a prolonged dry spell.

Creating Humus

The best thing to do with your grass clippings is to leave them on the lawn where they'll eventually decompose into valuable humus and return to the top inch or so of the surface of the soil. Of course, if you let the grass get 3 or 4 inches (7.5 or 10 cm) long before mowing, you'll need to rake up the clippings and consign them to the home garden compost factory or use them as a valuable mulch around your evergreens, rose bushes or vegetables. Such clippings, if left on the lawn, would smother the grass plants.

Never burn grass clippings or dispose of them in the garbage can. It took plant food and energy in the soil to produce them and if you put

1. Ajuga or
bugleweed.

2. Vinca minor.

3. Japanese spurge
or pachysandra.

J.L. EGGENS

70

1. Ivy.

2. Ivy.

3. Hosta or
plantain lilies.

71

them in the garbage or burn them you'll have taken something from the earth that will never be returned unless additional fertilizer and humus are applied.

The best thing for the home gardener to do with grass clippings and any other leafy material from the garden — faded cut flowers, weeds, lettuce leaves, cabbage and cauliflower leaves (not stems), citrus fruit skins, potato, turnip, carrot and similar peelings, tree leaves (with the exception of oak) etc. — is to place them in the home garden compost factory.

The Home Compost Factory

For gardening on a large or small scale, a home compost factory is a must. Here, you can turn any leafy material (grass clippings, spent flowers, weeds, leaves from vegetables, skins of citrus fruits, peelings from potatoes, turnips, carrots, beets, etc., and leaves from trees or shrubs) into valuable humus at almost no cost.

I should note here that, contrary to popular opinion, no undesirable odor will be generated by your compost box and it won't attract any vermin such as rats and mice. The process is a completely clean and natural one which has been going on since time began — just take a walk in the woods and you'll see the same composting process continually taking place under the trees.

Making a home compost factory is neither difficult nor expensive. For the average lawn or garden, a box 6 feet (1.8 m) long by 4 feet (1.2 m) wide, and 4 to 6 feet (1.2 to 1.8 m) deep would be the correct size. It won't require either a bottom or a top. Some people with large gardens like to have two boxes side by side. The enclosed end and the sides can be made of any rough lumber that's available. A visit to a wrecker can be an inexpensive way of obtaining the wood you need. Plaster laths, snow fencing or concrete blocks can also be used but most people make the box out of wooden boards. If you follow this method, it's wise to paint the boards inside and out with copper waterproofing paint. This will help prevent the lumber from rotting too quickly, and considerably prolong the life of your compost factory. The outside of the box can be coated with a second layer of outdoor paint to match the house or garage.

If you start adding material to the box in early spring, you'll have a substantial supply of excellent humus to dig into the soil by fall. It is possible, however, to make usable compost in 3 to 4 weeks if you can't wait the normal 4 to 6 months.

A special cutting blade which fits any rotary mower and which finely grinds all the material to be made into humus has recently been introduced to the marketplace. The resulting mixture is placed in special plastic bags whose air cells permit the material to breathe. I've made satisfactory compost in a week using this new method.

University of California scientists have proven that a heat build-up in the center of the compost pile is all-important to quick composting. If you're adding grass clippings, cabbage leaves or other green material, you should mix some tougher material with them, such as weeds, straw, and dry leaves. The best plan is to pregrind any of the trash materials so that the particles are about an inch (2.5 cm) in diameter at the maximum. This will ensure that the heat build-up in the center of the box will quickly reach the level which encourages the hard-working bacteria to flourish.

A compost factory that's too shallow will not do the job because there isn't enough space for trash to insulate it and prevent the loss of heat. Researchers have found that 4 to 6 feet (1.2 to 1.8 m) is the optimum height for this purpose. As the trash is converted to humus, the pile will shrink to about 3 feet (1 m).

The trash material must be moist at all times, but not so wet that oxygen is prevented from circulating. Green refuse such as cabbage and lettuce leaves need no water at all in the beginning, but dry leaves, stalks and grass clippings should be dampened as they are added to the pile. The moisture contained in the entire pile should be no more than you could squeeze out of the average sponge.

For quick composting the material should be turned every 3 or 4 days. This will aerate the compost, give you a chance to adjust the moisture level, and allow the bacteria access to the trash that was on the outside of the pile. If you're not interested in speeding up the natural process, turning the material once a month will be sufficient.

Faster and better composting can also be achieved by covering the home garden factory with black plastic. This greatly increases the heat build-up in the center of the pile by attracting the sun and helping to retain its warmth.

Start your home garden compost by adding material and tramping it down until you have a layer about 6 inches (15 cm) deep. Adjust the moisture level and then cover this first layer with one inch (25 mm) of top soil to improve the texture of the humus. Start a second layer on top and continue in the same manner until the compost box is filled.

August

In early August give the lawn another feeding with one of the complete lawn fertilizers high in nitrogen. Quite often a new crop of broadleaved weeds appears in the lawn at this time. If that's the case, apply one of the complete lawn fertilizers which has been combined with one or more forms of 2,4-D.

Seed or Sod?

The most important lawn chore in August is to seed a new lawn. There are two times during the year to sow a new lawn. One is just as soon as the soil is workable in the spring. The other, which is by far the best, is during the 4 week period starting the 15th of August. Late summer is the most suitable time because there are very few ups and downs in temperature during this period of the growing season. It's also the time when Mother Nature sows her own grasses and you can never go far wrong when you imitate her methods.

However, it's not always possible to wait until late summer to sow a lawn. Anyone just moving into a new home in the spring isn't prepared to wait until the middle of August to have the ground covered with a bright green carpet. This is particularly true of young couples with small children. For them, there's simply no way of waiting until the middle of August to get a lawn underway.

Fortunately, a spring sowing can be very successful, providing you get it done in the 3 or 4 week period immediately after the ground becomes workable in the spring. Seeding time will vary with the local climate but in most areas this would be some time between the last week in April and the first week in June.

The other answer to the problem would be to lay down sod. Whether to seed or sod a new lawn is a question which puzzles many new home owners. The cost of preparing and levelling the soil is the same for sodding or seeding. For most people the deciding factor is the extra cost of sod, balanced against the immediate lawn you get by using it.

75

Nursery sod has only been generally available for the past 15 years or so. Before that, its use was limited to providing quick ground cover or a temporary lawn. This was because the sod came from old pastures whose grasses were never satisfactory for lawn purposes in the first place and, in the second place, was invariably full of weeds and grasses of the worst kind. Nursery sod is now available to almost anyone living in Canada and the United States. Sodding can be carried out from the time sod becomes available in the spring until as late as the first of November in the warmer areas.

Preparing for the New Lawn

The same preparation is required whether you plan to use seed or put down sod. No other operation in gardening requires more care than preparing the soil for making a first-class lawn. Once a layer of turf is established either by seeding or sodding, you shouldn't have to disturb it in your lifetime. There are records of English lawns which have been unturned and undisturbed for over 300 years.

The First Step

The first step in making a new lawn, is to push to one side the existing 7 or 8 inches (18 or 20 cm) top soil and place it in piles. If you're using the services of a landscaping contractor, make sure you're there when this is being done so that every square yard of top soil is saved. It's taken nature a million or more years to develop the top soil, and it's worth the effort on your part to preserve it.

Grading

When constructing a new lawn, the foundation walls and the sides and the front and rear of the garden are the fixed grade points. The purpose of grading the subsoil is to arrange the ground between these fixed points in gentle pleasant slopes which will lead any excess water away from the house and, eventually, off the property. If, for example, you or the landscape contractor are careless and have the soil sloping a little towards the home, you'll discover to your dismay that a small lake will develop close to the foundation wall at certain times of the year. There's hardly anything you can do to prevent that water from then seeping through the walls into the cellar. Building experts will tell you that one of the main causes of moisture leaking in through basement walls is the accumulation of excess water alongside them.

Except for special locations, where the house may be constructed on the side of a hill, it doesn't pay to mound up the earth around it in terraces. These give your house the appearance of being pushed up off the ground and prevent it from blending naturally into the landscape.

76

Levelling

After grading, you will need to smooth the bumps and hollows in the subsoil. I can't emphasize too strongly the importance of this step in the preparation of a new lawn. If you do not eliminate all bumps now, they will appear in the finished lawn, not only spoiling its appearance but causing a great deal of trouble with the lawn mower later on.

Top Soil

Once you've established the correct grade and eliminated the bumps and hollows in the subsoil, the next job is to put the reserved top soil back in place. Then add some humus and fertilizer to improve it. Keep in mind that once a lawn is in place, either by sodding or seeding, there's very little you can do to improve it except by following a correct lawn fertilizer feeding program and possibly top-dressing with sterilized top soil from time to time.

High quality top soil is essential. There are very few building lots that contain the kind of soil needed to sod or seed a new lawn, nor are they suitable for constructing the various flower beds and foundations that you may require. Neither is it economically practical for many people to go out and buy the good top soil needed, so they're faced with improving the existing earth.

The main ingredients you'll need to add are humus, phosphorus and, to a lesser extent, potash. I readily admit that lawn grasses do help form some of their own humus when the old grass roots die and rot down, and the grass clippings decompose and enter the surface of the earth, but that doesn't mean you can ignore the necessity of adding a large supply of humus to the top soil when preparing to lay sod or sow seed.

The following forms of humus are excellent for this purpose: composted cattle manure, peat moss, discarded mushroom manure, horse manure one year old, or material from the home garden compost factory. Once the top soil has been put back in place and the surface of the earth is graded correctly, scatter a layer of humus over it 3 inches (7.5 cm) deep. The kind you use will depend on its availability and cost.

The most critical plant food element which must be added to the soil in preparation for a new lawn is phosphorus. One generous application of phosphorus can feed the grass plants with its goodness for as long as 50 years. That's why I recommend applying 2 fertilizers over the humus at this time. First of all, scatter a complete lawn fertilizer high in nitrogen, at five pounds (2.3 kg) per 1,000 square feet (17.5 square meters) or at the rate suggested by the manufacturer. Then apply an additional 25 pounds (11 kg) of superphosphate. Both kinds of fertilizer and the humus should be thoroughly mixed with the soil down to a

77

depth of at least 6 inches (15 cm) by using a rotary tiller which can be obtained from a rent-all store.

At this point the lawn is raked 3 or 4 times to level the surface and to remove any sticks, stones, bones and other debris which may have been thrown up by the rotary tiller.

Grass Seeds and Seeding

New and tremendously improved varieties of grass seed are gradually becoming available to home gardeners. There are literally hundreds of species of grasses which thrive in temperate areas, but very few of them will persist for any length of time and grow well under the artificial conditions of modern lawn management.

The best types of lawn grasses for temperate regions include the Kentucky bluegrasses, fine fescues such as Creeping Red and Chewings and the bent grasses which have specialized uses for golf and bowling greens.

Until recently, most commercial seed sold for lawn use originated from grasses not selected or bred for lawn purposes, but for farm use in hay and pasture fields. Grass plants produced from such seed tend to have an undesirable upright habit of growth, form a loose open turf, and are all too often susceptible to lawn grass leaf diseases. Weeds can easily invade such lawns and the grass plants don't stand mowing well.

The first good variety of grass seed to be introduced after the end of World War II was Merion, a special form of Kentucky bluegrass. There's no doubt that it's been an excellent variety and has been widely used for home gardens in the temperate parts of Canada and the United States. Unfortunately, it's susceptible to some of the more serious lawn grass diseases such as mildew, rust and striped smut. It also doesn't grow well under shady conditions and requires a large amount of fertilizer to keep it thriving.

There are now excellent turf grass testing programs at a large number of research stations and universities in North America. I recently visited one of the largest of these and found more than 300 new varieties from both North American and European breeders being tested. All this breeding, testing and research means that dozens of excellent new turf grasses will be marketed in the next few years. They will not only have a more attractive appearance and maximum resistance to disease, but will also require less fertilizer.

The new grasses will have a built-in resistance to such diseases as rust, snowmold, mildew, striped smut and leafspot. They'll have a shorter, compact habit of growth and good sod-forming ability. Such grasses will have strong creeping characteristics and will knit together to keep out the weeds. They'll have good color, be winter-hardy, and

78

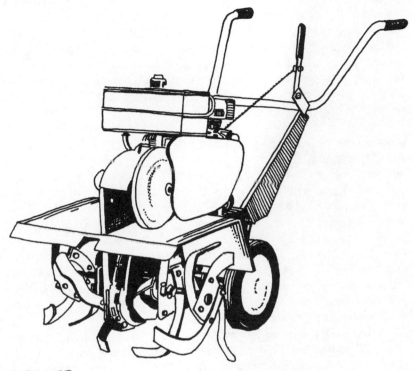

ROTOTILLER

have remarkable shade and drought resistance. One can expect them to exhibit the same excellent growth qualities that we've come to expect from hybrid flowers and vegetables.

In purchasing lawn seed, it always pays to buy the best quality mixture available, regardless of the price. There's still a great difference in the quality of the lawn grass mixtures being sold today. Part of the problem lies in the type of grasses used to make up the mixture. The cheaper ones contain more of the coarser, large-seeded kinds of grass which germinate quickly but don't last very long in the lawn. To give you an example, 1 pound (400 gm) of annual ryegrass contains about 200,000 seeds, while a similar amount of Kentucky bluegrass will consist of over 2,000,000. Ryegrass is much cheaper than Kentucky bluegrass, and the more of it that's in the mixture, the less they have to charge for it. It seldom lasts over the first winter, and while it's growing tends to compete with, and crowd out, the more desirable strains such as the bluegrasses, and the fine fescues.

In both Canada and the United States there's a definite trend towards improving lawn grass mixtures, not only with regard to the mechanical mixing of seeds, but with use of newer and better varieties. At the moment, you can be sure that, if you buy one of the cheaper mixtures, you'll also be receiving a fair number of weed seeds. However, the producers of the newer and better mixtures have attempted to completely eliminate weed seeds. That's why it's so important to buy only the high quality kinds.

The best mixtures contain a much higher proportion of the fine seeded grasses, such as Kentucky bluegrass and fescues, which means they'll go much further. So much further, in fact, that the mixture which sells for the most money by weight is probably the cheapest in the end. A pound (400 gm) of such a mixture will cover twice the lawn area as many of the so-called cheaper mixtures. Obviously, it pays to estimate the cost on the basis of area covered, not by weight.

Keep in mind also that the price of the seed is but a very small fraction of the cost of establishing a new lawn, when you take into account the grading, improving the top soil, the fertilizer, and the labor required. It makes good gardening sense to buy the seed that will best create the ideal, permanent lawn which won't have to be re-sown every 3 or 4 years.

After giving the lawn surface its final raking, it's time to sow the seed. If you buy a first-class grass seed mixture, you'll only need 3 pounds (1.4 kg) per 1,000 square feet (17.5 square meters) of lawn area, whereas if you opt for a cheap one you'll need 5 pounds (2.3 kg) to cover the same area.

Seeding must be uniform or there'll be an uneven pattern to the turf and bare spots will be created. A fertilizer spreader or a cyclone seeder is the best way of making sure the seed is applied uniformly. Divide the seed in half, sowing one part one way and the other at right angles to it.

After the seed is sown rake the soil lightly, using just the tip of the rake. At the same time, make sure you only cover the seeds about 1/8 inch (3 mm) deep. If you cover the seeds much deeper then chances are they won't germinate.

Just as soon as you've sown the seed and raked the surface of the new lawn you'll need to roll it with an empty roller to firm the ground and remove any little humps and footprints. Do this when the ground is dry so that the seed and soil will not stick to the roller. The newly sown lawn should be given a gentle but thorough watering immediately after the rolling and raking has been completed. Grass seed must be moist before it will start to germinate. From then on you must never let the lawn dry out or few, if any, of the seeds will germinate. These early waterings, like all those to be applied in the future, must be thorough but applied gently enough to avoid washing the soil and seed away. Try to water from the sides of the lawn so that you won't need to drag the hose across the freshly sown seed.

Don't worry when you see birds helping themselves to the lawn grass seeds. The amount they'll consume is almost never serious. A mixture of first class lawn grasses will contain over 2,000,000 seeds per pound (400 g). If all these were to germinate you'd have far too many grass plants.

It will most likely be 4 or 5 weeks before the new lawn will need mowing for the first time. The young, tender growth of the new lawn is bound to be as soft and succulent as it is in the early spring. The moisture content will be much higher than that of mature grass. This means that the grass of the new lawn must be cut with a sharp, well-adjusted mower to avoid damage. Wait until the new grass plants are 3 inches (7.5 cm) high before doing the first mowing. Have the mower set so that it will cut 2 inches (5 cm) high. At no time should more than 1/4 to 1/3 of the total leaf surface be removed at one time.

From this time on, mow once a week until the grass plants stop growing. For the final mowing of the season set the blade so that it will cut the grass 1 inch (2.5 cm) high.

Fall and Winter

During the last week in September or the first 10 days of October new and established lawns are given the second most important feeding of the season. A popular misconception is that fall-fed lawns are stimulated into soft growth and enter into winter in a tender state, with resultant winter killing. As a direct result of this faulty reasoning many home gardeners don't fertilize in late September or early October which is perhaps the most critical period of the year.

Unlike trees and shrubs, hardy lawn grasses have no cabium layer to be killed by freezing, nor do they go fully dormant. Instead, they're able to start into growth again at any time after soil and air temperatures go above 32°F (0°C), even for short periods during January and February thaws. Growth is very slow but it does occur, mainly in the root zone.

In the fall, instead of producing soft top growth, fertilizers are used to develop rhizomes and tillers which are needed by the plants as storage organs. This results in fall-fed lawns having deeper, huskier roots and being more drought resistant.

There's an interesting reason why root growth is stimulated by fall feeding. Careful scientific tests show that the red light of the spectrum has no effect on top growth but does stimulate root growth. As the sun sinks lower and lower in the southern sky with the arrival of autumn, it must pass through more and more air. This screens out the weaker blue rays needed for top growth, but allows the longer red rays to come through. At this time most of the old roots begin to die off and are replaced by new ones. Thus, fall-fed lawns build up a strong root system without soft, lush top growth. In this way the balance between top and root growth becomes much better than when soft, lush blades are forced in the spring without a corresponding increase in the root area.

All this means that it is necessary to apply a fertilizer specially formulated to fill the needs of the lawn until the grass plants stop

MALAK

83

growing and, at the same time, to help them withstand the onslaught of winter cold. A feeding at this time will help the grass plants to continue and expand their newly developing root systems. This process goes on for much longer than one would expect, even after the first crust of frozen soil covers the surface of the lawn in late fall or early winter.

In many gardens, as growth slows up in the fall, the home owner does not mow as frequently and allows the grass to grow too long. This produces a tangled mat of dead organic matter under which summer turf disease organisms survive (some in the form of dormant spores.) This gives the winter snow mold fungi a chance to multiply rapidly.

Keep the lawn mown once a week until the grass plants stop growing for the season and then adjust the mower so that it will cut the grass 1 inch (2.5 cm) high for the final mowing of the season. This will prevent the grass plants from smothering and save trouble from several potentially serious turf diseases next year.

Just as soon as the final mowing is finished take the mower for sharpening and servicing. If you wait until the grass has started to grow next spring you probably won't get your mower back in time for the all important first mowing of the season.

Lawn Diseases

Rust

Many lawns can be attacked by rust fungi without the home gardener realizing it. Unfortunately, the ravages and evidence of the disease are concealed in the late summer because many of the leaves are already brown from drought and other causes. Rust usually appears in late summer when heavy dew aids its development.

About 10 days after the spores have infected the leaves, lesions will start to appear. Yellowish-orange or reddish-brown spots develop on the leaves. If a cloth is rubbed across the infected leaves, the rust-colored spores adhere to it and produce a yellow or orange stain.

Rust isn't a fatal disease, but it can be serious on turf that has stopped growing through lack of moisture and plant food.

To control the disease once it appears you must first feed the lawn with a complete fertilizer high in nitrogen, then water it thoroughly to promote new growth. Mow and remove all the cuttings. Treat the rust-infested areas with a lawn fungicide; the nursery or garden center will be able to recommend the correct one. Make 2 applications 10 days apart to break the rust cycle.

Leaf Spot

Leaf spot is probably the most widespread and destructive of the fungus diseases that attack grass plants. It's particularly damaging to the leaves and stems, and appears in the form of reddish-brown to purplish-black spots. They cause the leaves to shrivel and the stems, crowns and roots to discolor and rot. Infected grass plants are often thought to have been killed by dry weather when in reality they're victims of leaf spot.

One of the best ways of controlling the disease is to use one of the newer lawn grasses which have been bred to be resistant to leaf spot. When mowing the lawn be sure to set the lawn mower so that it will cut the grass 2 inches (5 cm) high. Follow a regular lawn feeding program, applying enough of the complete fertilizer high in nitrogen to keep the grass healthy and thriving.

Treat the infected areas with a lawn fungicide and remove the grass clippings after each mowing.

Snow Mold: A Winter Disease of Lawns

Snow mold is often called "winter killing" by many home gardeners but it is really a fungus disease which appears when the snow melts. When the lawn begins to grow in the spring it shows up as patches of dead grass surrounded by green.

Contrary to some theories, snow is not essential to development of this mold, although snow does supply constant moisture and shade which favor the development of the causative fungi. Several different types of fungus can cause snow mold which is why the dead patches can be oyster white, beige, grey, tan or pinkish grey. The spores survive the summer lying dormant in mats of dead organic matter that have accumulated on lawn surfaces because of the clippings. These organisms become active only when, in the fall, temperatures drop below 40°F (4°C) for several days. A covering of snow provides ideal conditions for growth.

Unless the grass roots have been killed, snow mold patches should recover without treatment. However, since conditions favoring their development also favor leaf spot and other summer turf diseases, a spraying in the spring when the grass plants have started to grow is recommended to prevent further trouble. If the summer is rainy, pink snow mold can attack the grass plants in the hot weather of July and August.

Sanitation is just as important as chemical control. The first step is to deprive the fungi that cause snow mold of the dead organic matter in which they survive. A vigorous raking will help, but the use of a mechanical turf renovator such as the Verticut or a powered rake will do the job better and in 1/10 the time. These units can usually be obtained from rent-all stores and the better garden centers and nurseries.

85

DAVE MALLOCH

1. *Leaf spot.*

2. *Snow mold.*

J.L. EGGENS

3. *Striped smut*
   [*close-up*].

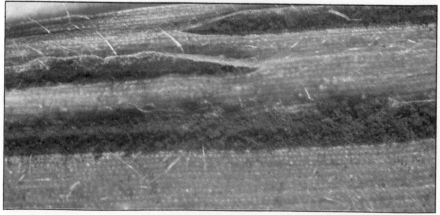

DAVE MALLOCH

86

DAVE MALLOCH

1. Slime mold.

J.L. EGGENS

2. Snow mold
   [close-up].

3. Moss in lawn.

J.L. EGGENS

87

Keep mowing the grass as long as it keeps growing in the fall. Remove the clippings and rake off the fallen leaves quickly. Don't use a mulching attachment on a rotary mower to grind up leaves because the resulting mulch is a perfect snow mold incubator.

Avoid the use of organic fertilizers. These always contain starches and sugars that feed the snow mold fungi more than they feed the grass. This means not using sewage sludge, composted cattle and sheep manures, cottonseed meal and so on. The best thing to use is straight chemical lawn fertilizers high in nitrogen. Peat moss, however, is safe to use because it has already been digested by soil bacteria and no longer contains available starches and sugars.

To prevent snow mold in the fall, spray the turf with a lawn fungicide after the first few light freezes.

Powdery Mildew

Powdery mildew is a fungus disease which starts to appear on the grass leaves with the arrival of the cooler temperatures and more frequent rains of late summer and early autumn. You can suspect mildew if the grass leaves look like they are covered with a faint skim of hoar frost or as if a coat of whitewash had been applied to them.

This fungus disease makes its appearance in the shaded areas first, then spreads to the rest of the lawn in severe attacks. To be perfectly honest, it's usually more unsightly than it is harmful to the grass plants. The cheapest and quickest remedy is to dust with sulphur, applied as recommended by the manufacturer. Sulphur gets rid of the mildew fungus spores in active growth at the time, but has little residual effect. However, since the mildew season comes to an end in September, sulphur is worth using in place of more costly, longer-lasting materials.

Slime Molds

It doesn't happen very often, but during wet weather you may discover slime molds covering areas of grass with a dusty bluish-grey, black or yellow mass. Luckily, they're not parasitic but they are extremely unpleasant. As these molds feed on dead organic matter, the most damage they can do to the grass plants is to shade and discolor the blades. This type of mold will rapidly disappear when the weather turns dry.

Usually, the masses can be easily broken up either by hitting them with a strong stream of water from the hose or by sweeping them with a kitchen broom. During an abnormally long spell of wet weather, these slime molds can be especially annoying. In such cases the best thing to do is to apply a lawn fungicide to the affected areas.

Moss in the Lawn

When green moss appears in the lawn many home gardeners blame a lack of lime in the soil. Nothing could be further from the truth in the case of most lawns where it appears. The real culprit is, almost without exception, a lack of plant food. In isolated cases, the moss can be the result of poor drainage and high acidity but in most lawns a regular lawn feeding program will rectify the condition.

Control starts with a good raking to remove most of the moss. Care should be taken not to rake too vigorously, otherwise many of the grass plants can be pulled up by the roots. One of the fan-shaped bamboo or aluminum lightweight rakes is best for this purpose. Follow up the raking with a feeding of complete lawn fertilizer high in nitrogen, at the rate recommended by the manufacturer.

Any of the resulting bare spots should be repaired by following the information given earlier in the book under "Repairing Bare Spots". Be assured that a regular lawn feeding program throughout the gardening season will usually keep moss out of the lawn as it doesn't flourish in rich earth.

The Modern Lawn

How to Choose Lawnseed

Better than most consumer products, a package of grass seed clearly indicates the quality of its blend. While the home gardener must decide for himself what type of grass he wishes to grow, the label on a seed package will tell him not only if the varieties he has chosen are contained in the blend, but in what quantity. It effectively rates the blend in terms of purity, by giving the ratio of desirable to undesirable varieties of seed.

The inexperienced gardener in particular may benefit from the modern labelling system, which identifies grasses as either coarse or fine-textured. The most attractive lawn grasses fall into the second category; they make a much more attractive and satisfactory turf than do the coarse field grasses. So, right away, much of the mystery has been taken out of buying lawn seed simply by reading the label. For example, you can be assured that a seed blend which is made up en-

Kentucky bluegrass.

Red fescue.

J.L. EGGENS

MALAK

91

tirely of fine-textured varieties will produce a lawn free of rank, unsightly grasses.

As yet, no one has created a special grass that will grow well in the shade. The best solution to low-light conditions is to choose a seed mixture containing a large proportion of the various fescues which are much more tolerant of shade than the bluegrasses. Keep in mind that if your lawn will receive only 25 per cent or less full sunlight, no lawnseed mixture will be able to provide satisfactory results for any length of time. In such cases, you are far better off using a perennial ground cover such as Ajuga, Pachysandra or Vinca.

Fine-Textured Grasses

Some years ago, after much deliberation, authorities agreed that certain grasses would be termed fine-textured. Three basic types of grasses fit into this category:

1. All of the Kentucky bluegrasses, the most prominent varieties being Baron, Sydsport, Adelphi, Burka, Nugget, Haga, Ram I, Touchdown, Majestic, and Cherie.

2. The fine or red fescues such as Chewing, Highlight, Coquette, Jamestown, Pennlawn, and Barfala.

3. The fairly new perennial rye grasses which germinate in 7 days. They are fine-stemmed and almost the same color as Kentucky bluegrass, and include Manhattan, Pennfine, Derby, Omega, and Yorktown II.

Blends

Planting blends of grass seed has a number of advantages over planting a single variety. With a mixture of seeds you avoid having "all your eggs in one basket" and lower the risk of losing your entire lawn to disease. Seldom are differing grasses, or even cultivars of the same variety, victims of the same disease. For this reason, suppliers of lawn seed generally combine several grasses in one blend. Most of the time, two or more varieties of Kentucky bluegrass will be mixed with one or two fine fescues, in proportions suited to the local climate and soil.

With blends, the percentage of each grass variety is always listed on the label. There's nothing perplexing about these figures and they're a simple means of determining whether you're buying a first-class lawnseed mixture or an inferior one. Obviously if the label says there is a high percentage of a select variety of grass, the seed is more valuable. On the other hand, there are the so-called "bargain" mixtures which contain very low percentages of some highly desirable grasses but whose brand names would indicate otherwise. For example, when Baron Kentucky bluegrass was quite expensive, Baron mixtures were being marketed which actually contained as little as 1 per cent Baron Kentucky seeds.

Coarse Grasses

Annual ryegrass is a frequent component of inexpensive mixtures. While it does sprout quickly, it generally won't survive into the second year. Even if some plants survive in favored locations they become quite coarse and clumpy. However, annual ryegrass and Redtop may be useful, in small percentages, as nursegrasses in locations such as a newly seeded slope. Other coarse grasses, like Timothy, Orchardgrass or Bromograss, have little usefulness in a lawn. Neither do legumes, such as white clover, which are better sown separately if they are required.

A relatively new development in North American lawn seed is the fine-textured "turf-type" perennial ryegrasses. These provide the quick growing qualities of annual ryegrass with the longevity, winter-hardiness and much improved color of the Kentucky bluegrasses.

In colder areas, there perennial ryegrasses don't have the staying power of the bluegrasses and fescues, but they should last for 4 or 5 years. They will germinate in 7 days, in contrast to the bluegrasses which take up to a month. A mixture of 70 per cent perennial ryegrasses and 30 per cent Kentucky bluegrass is excellent. Two months after sowing, the ryegrasses will have produced an ideal lawn. As these grasses begin to thin 3 or 4 years later, the bluegrass will take over.

Coated Grass Seed

Coated grass seed is now generally available and is a great help in establishing a new lawn. The coating contains phosphorus which promotes early and vigorous growth and, at the same time, prevents fertilizer burn. Coated grass seed may be mixed with a complete lawn fertilizer high in nitrogen, and the two ingredients can be sown in one application. In addition, the colored seed is easier to see, reducing the chance of overlapping, and insects and birds don't recognize it as food. This valuable coating technique was first developed in New Zealand where the seeding of forage grasses in isolated areas had to be carried out by airplane. The coated seed has since been extensively tested in the United States and Canada and has proven to be quite beneficial in the production of healthier, more dense stands of lawn grass.

Bluegrass plant showing healthy rhizome growth.

Properly fertilized Kentucky bluegrass root system.

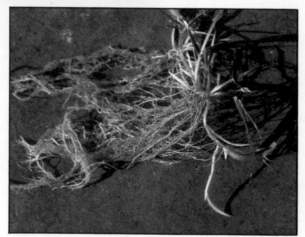

J.L. EGGENS

Grass Patch

One of the newest and most useful products on the market is Grass Patch. At one time or another, most lawns develop bare or brown spots. Whether the problem is caused by dogs, rodents, diseases or winter kill, this new product can easily solve it. It combines a blend of perennial rye and bluegrass seeds and supplements them with enzymes, a moisture retainer, and organic additives. All you have to do is to scratch the surface of the soil with a rake or fork and apply a small handful of Grass Patch, covering the surface of the spot. Water it gently every day until the perennial ryegrass seeds begin to germinate, usually in 6 or 7 days. Within 3 or 4 weeks the ugly brown spots or bare patches will have been repaired.

94

Index

Numbers in italic indicate pages on which illustrations occur.

For further information about forthcoming Bradshaw Gardening Guides, Bradshaw Gardening Booklets, and Bradshaw Gardening Aids, please write to:

John Bradshaw
25 Hollinger Road
Toronto, Ontario
M4B 3G2